# THE RIGHT TO BE HAPPY

"Good wine needs no bush, and good morals no bated breath."

*Sayings of Lo Su*

"Children go to school impressed with the belief that they have a right to be happy, that God will give them a good time. This is the perversion of true religion, self-denial and obedience."

THE HON. AND REV. E. LYTTELTON (Ex-Headmaster of Eton), in *The Evening Standard*, Oct. 14th, 1925

# THE RIGHT
# TO BE HAPPY

BY

MRS BERTRAND RUSSELL
(DORA RUSSELL)

NEW YORK *and* LONDON
Harper & Brothers Publishers
*MCMXXVII*

# PREFACE

THIS book attempts two things : first to demonstrate that happiness for all human beings is not only feasible, but the most satisfactory basis for social construction ; second to bring to the help of such construction modern theories of the nature of man and the universe. At a time when there is so widespread a struggle against national, class, and sexual oppression, it seems important to examine the various claims which are advanced, and to see whether, after all, there is not behind them a consistent new philosophy.

To me at least it appears that people of our time are expressing new ethics and metaphysics against which the old ones may be weighed and found wanting. Such views, however, lie scattered among specialists in the various sciences, in education, and psychology, or are confusedly shouted as slogans of party or sex. We suffer very much in England and America from the rigid separation of thought in the various departments of life. In Russia an attempt at a constructive modern synthesis has been made, and—though this will be displeasing both to the reactionary and revolutionary American—it seems to me that metaphysics and psychology in America are building an intellectual, though not as yet a political, synthesis that is almost identical with that of Soviet Russia. I call this the mechanical synthesis. Newton and Descartes laid the foundations of its metaphysic and Professor Watson has given the latest and most revolutionary expression to its psychology. This synthesis is useful in that it affords hypotheses helpful to scientific discovery ; it is harmful when it is accepted as a dogma. As such it does seem to be too frequently accepted, and to be superseding the old medieval sanctions—to which on the whole it is preferable. But dogmas based on mechanics will not solve all human problems or successfully promote human happiness. It is significant that both Professor Watson and the Bolsheviks are united in their hearty contempt for heredity and biological sanctions. They are somewhat remote from agriculture and they like to think that men and human society can be re-made like a machine to suit a definite plan in their minds. Professor Watson allows the merest germ of inborn instinct or nature : the rest of the human creature he holds to be manufactured by the " conditioning of his reactions ". The *criteria* by which he—or the Bolsheviks—would judge completed individuals are reminiscent of industrial organization : efficiency in action and quantity in output. Professor Watson, for whose work I have in many respects the profoundest admiration, comes, in the final chapter of *Behaviourism*, to some curious conclusions, which, however, flow quite logically from his general thesis. He measures the value of a writer by the amount he is paid per word ; in business he has the typical hustler's outlook ; and the value of a picture seems to depend in his opinion on the number of people who admire it.

Far be it from me or anyone in this tortured age to suggest that it would not be well to re-create society. The world as we know it is a hideous nightmare. Human beings have made it, and therefore human beings need to be changed. The chemistry of the human body and the study of human reactions can give us the means of going beyond changes of environment to changes in the nature of the human creature himself. I quarrel merely with the idea of a plan, according to which all men are at once to be made anew. The medievalists had such a plan. We were born in sin, and re-born into the Kingdom of Heaven, with the result that it became intolerable to us to go on living upon the earth. It has taken us centuries of thought and mockery to shake the medieval system ; thought and mockery here and now are required to prevent the mechanists from building another. Without falling into a mystical vitalism that reverences organic nature as sacred, we can at least try rather to serve than to subdue the prancing seas of life. With this in view I have taken as impulses, instincts, or needs, certain driving forces in the human species as we know it at present, and argued for such social and economic changes as will give them new, free, and varied expression. To take even this first step towards a happy society is a herculean task. After it has been accomplished generations to come will see

# PREFACE

what the creature will do next.  We none of us know ; and we should be thoroughly on our guard against all those who pretend that they do.

DORA RUSSELL.

CARN VOEL,
   PORTHCURNO, CORNWALL.

# CONTENTS

# CONTENTS

# THE RIGHT TO BE HAPPY

# IMMORTALITY

Blue, white, grey are the clouds
And patches of grey and silver are made on the
sea ;
And paths of blue and pearl for the ships to go.

Blue, white, grey is the house
I have made on the hilltop,
Where the clouds shall go over and winds shall
blow
And we shall gaze on the sea.
Children and lawns and flowers shall blossom
about us.

When we die
May we sleep in love ;
Perhaps in the winds our thoughts will speak to
our children.
Let people say
They were fearless in life and loved beauty,
Therefore these souls are worthy
To cleanse and ride with the majestic sea
And to speak and wander the world with the
murmuring winds.

# THE RIGHT TO BE HAPPY

## I

### CONCEPTIONS OF LIFE

#### CHINESE, GREEKS, AND CHRISTIANS

Happiness is so rare an achievement in the modern world and the means to acquire it seem so simple, that the superficial observer may be excused for crying out at the contrariness of human beings.

A closer examination, however, would convince anyone capable of some degree of scientific impartiality that the application of these simple rules to the world in its present state would involve the most surprising upheavals and explosions. Possibly these would be so great as still further to destroy the chance of happiness for several generations. If that is so, whoever desires human happiness must seek to acquire neither the sword of the warrior nor the sanctimonious rhetoric of a preacher, but rather the pen of persuasion and the tongue of the weary mother gently conquering the turbulent impulses of her child. He must have fires that are held in check that they may neither alarm nor anger his hearers, and a wit that is apt and quick to prick bubbles but never so quick nor so malign that the over-indignant bubble-worshipper turns at once to inflate his angry cheeks in the creation of another idol. These qualities are demanded, and the writer of this book lays no claim to their possession. A preliminary examination of the problem is all that she proposes. But if there were in every country of the world a mere handful of men and women with mental and physical habits adapted to the needs of the modern world and if they possessed courage, eloquence and wit both in the spoken and the written word, they might without decay and disaster lay the foundations of a future radiant with happiness for all mankind.

It would not be necessary for such people to govern : the capture of opinion and the creation of a philosophy is their task. Nor would it be sufficient that they should merely dream and communicate their dreams to others.

The printing of an idea and its adoption by a chosen few does not mark the end of that idea's uses. Too often when a nation or a class has achieved happiness and freedom, those who assisted in that achievement forget the multitudes left outside. Preoccupied with quality, they omit quantitative thought. On the other hand, those who desire the possibility of happiness for every human being in a large society or in the whole world are apt to neglect quality of life, which alone, whether possessed by the many or the few, gives significance to human activity. Our supposititious band of moderns, therefore—they are not to be called super-men or women—must be ready to demonstrate by the effortless grace of their lives and the harmony between their activity and their thought that they possess a view of life adequate to conquering their environment. More than that they must show in speech and action that this way of life can be practised by all and is capable of being the foundation of a society. It is only very partially true that society is built upon economic causes rather than ideas. The interaction of economic causes and of ideas in the building of social systems is an interesting study, but it is beyond question that a synthesis of thought or belief has immense power to hold groups together, even when that synthesis has been proved false, or its uses are outgrown.

Until the French Revolution human happiness as a basis for the theory of states was barely considered. The Greeks perhaps, gave it a limited and undemocratic expression, but in the main up till the eighteenth century in Europe the hedonists have been isolated groups of people occupied merely with individual ethical values and aims that had little relation to metaphysical, religious, or political speculation. The hedonist would discuss " pleasure ", " desire ", " contentment ", without relation to the outward circumstances of his life, just as the metaphysician in considering the existence or non-existence of matter was unaffected by the argument that if he stubbed his toe or banged his head he would soon know which way to decide that problem. None the less, hedonists of the past were usually men who were in a position to carry out their ideas of a good life, neither poverty nor tyranny hindering them from the delights of good food, drink,

6

books, love, pleasant surroundings which they claimed as necessities for happiness. They were out of touch with those stern " realities of life " that are always supposed to bring people to their senses.

For this reason and for others that lie deeper, Europe in the past did not turn to the theories of hedonists for a synthesis on which to build her society. It was on the contrary a religion of asceticism, suffering, poverty, and submission on which the states of Europe and their patriotisms were founded. This is not really surprising.

Most human beings seem to find it difficult to be happy by means of a mere handful of ethical rules which in themselves depend on artificial economic or political conditions. They demand a survey of the universe, a solution, or at the very least an interpretation of its boundless mysteries. Then again, our views of life are conditioned not only by our dreams and our desires, but by our powers. Men's ignorance and weakness in the face of natural forces formerly demanded a philosophy either of defiance or of resignation. Among the Greeks we find the story of Prometheus, stealing divine fire and hurling his challenge at the gods though they held him chained to a rock of torture. We find the *hubris* of Greek tragic heroes. Among the Christians resignation to suffering and death are compensated for by the splendour of the life to come in which a beneficent Father and His all-merciful Son unfold hidden secrets, heal wounds, and wipe away tears. Irrational beliefs have always been, and still are a substitute for knowledge, as resignation is the mark of impotent desires. The merit of Christianity as a way of life was that its outlook was democratic as between rich and poor, ignorant and intelligent, that it satisfied metaphysical longings and compensated for hardship and insecurity. Happiness on earth was a dream to which the fortunate few might attain, it could not in a world visited inexplicably by famine, plague, floods, and war, be the gospel of the many. The individual as he saw wife and children, friends and brothers pass one by one through the gate of death, kingdoms rise and fall, crops fail, fire and rain destroy apparently at the bidding of chance, cried out for comfort and could not find it except in some interpretation of that mystery. I think we may take it as certain that no view of life and no gospel of happiness has a chance of success that does not take a comprehensive view of human life and destiny. The first eighteenth century rationalists raised the cry of morals without religion, and the divines retorted that in destroying the Lawgiver they would destroy all laws. This is true in the sense that, illogical though it be, the mainspring of conduct whether of individuals or society is what is believed about the world. Beliefs may be irrational, or founded upon knowledge. Those who hold no beliefs are at the mercy of instinct. Indeed, instinct plays its part in a thousand ways which we shall hope to analyse.

The object of this and the following chapter is to disentangle the ethical and religious inheritance of the past and to compare and contrast the conditions which produced them with those that obtain to-day.

The three important influences which have shaped European metaphysics and morals are, roughly speaking, the Greek view of life, the Christian, and the influence of scientific thought and discovery. The conceptions of life prevailing in other continents have been so similar as to need no separate consideration, except possibly the ideas which govern Chinese civilization, for these differ in many respects from the conception of life commonly classed by the European as " Oriental ".

The Chinese view of life is remarkable for the absence of otherworldliness and asceticism, and of the extreme fierceness in persecution that accompany them. As a people the Chinese possess a quality of extreme rarity even in European individuals, the power of enduring suffering or disaster without the compensation of metaphysical or religious dreams. Their philosophy comes nearer to a rationalization of biological needs than anything we have invented. Through a period of pastoral and then agricultural civilization, they seem to have refused to fear or to make war upon material things or the life of instinct. Confronted by inevitable disasters of famine and flood, they are not defiant, nor do they cling to a dream of personal immortality for comfort. Their emotion flows along the natural instinctive channel, seeking honour and eternal life in their children and their children's children.

Their patriarchal feeling resembles that of the Jews ; possibly, like the Jews, they were fierce in nomadic times. However that may be, their tribal gods are lost in oblivion, and with them the sense of conflict or of God-given laws that set man at war with the universe. How it came about that the Chinese denied a philosophy of inert matter moved by a spirit or mind, and erected instead a theory of interpenetration, a sort of vitalism that colours their thought, their art, and their politics, does not seem to be known. It remains true that this philosophy has rendered them impervious to the doctrine of original sin, kept them free of sexual inhibitions, and preserved in them, till recent years, a wholesome contempt for the manufacture and use of industrial machinery. Women have suffered in China, as they have everywhere under the patriarchal system——their impulses and happiness a sacrifice to the certainty of paternal descent, but they have suffered less than in a system like our own, which, fundamentally patriarchal, cuts at its own heart by an ascetic denial of the biological necessities upon which it is based.

The view of life handed down to us by the best of Greek thought had in it greater dignity and potential happiness than any view of life that has yet prevailed in the world, with the possible exception of the Chinese. It was a view which gave opportunities to the intelligence of man, encouraging mathematical and scientific discovery and artistic effort. It did not dread instinctive delights, and valued supremely vigour and beauty of the body in both men and women. It does not seem to have been tormented by that antagonism between matter and the spirit which has been the scourge of Western civilization for nearly two thousand years. Even those who felt such an antagonism —as for instance, the Stoic philosophers— sought only to strike a balance between mental and bodily good. Though they looked to reason to control instinct, they did not aim at destroying instinct entirely, nor at escaping utterly from the tyranny of matter. Intelligence shaped matter, whether in artistic construction or in the conduct of life. Two things are missing in the Greek conception of life, a solution of which is demanded by every modern. Women, save with rare exceptions, shared only the instinctive but not the mental life of the community, and the problems of democracy and of work and leisure were avoided through the existence of an unprivileged slave population. Greek government was, indeed, a democracy, but a democracy wielded only by a class with opportunity for leisure. The Greeks, in fact, lay themselves open to the charge which can be brought against all the too comfortable hedonists that they led a sheltered existence. I mean by this that while they secured to Greek men in every sense of the phrase the right to be happy, they did not accord to Greek women or to their slaves a similar right. They cannot be said, therefore, to have settled the difficulties with which we are confronted, though they came nearer to it than we ourselves have done. For the manner in which the Greeks faced those disasters and difficulties from which there is no escape, we can have nothing but admiration. They refused to be intimidated by death and the forces of nature and the idea of God. They created their gods, but did not scruple to defy them or cause them to fight one against the other. The many gods of the Athenians, as

St. Paul well divined, were their safeguard against enslaving the spirit of man. For though they deified natural forces, they also deified the qualities of men and women. Gods and goddesses of wisdom, strength, courage in war, love, chastity, have their place beside those of the sea, the fruitful earth, the lightning and the storm. Agricultural and tribal religions mingle in the background of Greek thought, and no doubt had as dark and superstitious a hold upon the common people as Christianity in medieval Europe. But there is not, as in Christian countries, a synthesis supported by the cultured and intelligent section of the community. The life and achievements of man were on the whole more cherished by Greek thinkers than the tragedy of his mortality and failures.

Those more learned in Greek history than I will consider the above summary inadequate. It certainly is. But what matters for our present purpose is not the exact study of traditional conceptions, but the view of them which is current in popular thought. To popular European thought the Greeks stand for a surprising harmony between mental and physical activity such as has been rarely achieved in Europe since their time by individuals and still more rarely by communities. There was nothing in their code of ethics which denied the right of man to all forms of happiness, no sinister antagonisms, no cleaving of his life into two warring and irreconcilable halves. The very abuse of the " pagan " by the Christian has also implied a delight in life on the part of Greek or Roman which the Christian had learnt to despise. The " golden mean " as a way of life, which we attribute to Greek thinkers, has been the parent of all hedonistic ethics in Europe as their active intellect was the parent of our science.

The defeat of Greece and Rome by an ethical and religious synthesis which took root among their slaves was the natural consequence of building a social and political system on a basis of oppression. Bereft of rights, of happiness, and of security, men and women infallibly turn to morbid consolations. Starved of joy, they will infallibly end by exalting suffering, starved of knowledge they must needs worship at the shrine of virtuous ignorance. So much has been written on this subject that it is hardly necessary to stress the slave origin of European Christianity. Students are also familiar with the conclusions of scholars, who have traced in Christianity the tribal fierceness of Judaism wedded to the mysticism of agricultural rites. It is not out of place for our purpose to show briefly what this means in terms of individual ordinary life. Tribal ethics must inculcate some loyalty, some fierceness, and courage in hunting animals or enemies. The god of the tribe must be a warrior whose prowess in manipulating natural forces can bring victory. Thus did the God of the Jews make the sun to stand still at the uplifting of Joshua's hands. In savage life the prize is to the brave and enterprising, and such intelligence as the male possesses is bent on destruction, whether of the hunted prey or of a rival. Moreover, his warrior god, as anyone who reads the Old Testament must know, delights in the wholesale killing of men, women, children, flocks, and herds.

The life of the agriculturist calls for different virtues. Death presents itself to him rather as starvation than as the shaft of an enemy in battle. Darkness and winter appal him, his god must wield the sun, not to win battles, but to make the crops grow. As agriculture spreads throughout the earth, those who first teach it are mentioned in legend as the Children of the Sun.[1] It will readily be seen that patience, resignation, greater gentleness, contemplation, ultimately some feeling for the effort of creation come from this dependence on cultivation of the soil. It gives rise also to fierce cruelties and superstitions involving human sacrifice to propitiate the spirit of vegetation. It is significant, I think, that the emotion of fear in man when he lives by tilling the soil produces more morbid and paralysing effects than fear in the huntsman or warrior. To dread an equal tangible enemy brings a wholesome reaction of pugnacity, to dread a malevolent all-powerful spirit who will send hail or locusts or drought upon your crops inculcates cringing, subservience, readiness to pray and to sacrifice. The first is straightforward, the second an inhibited fear. Inhibited fears of this kind have played an enormous part in shaping religion and morality. Similarly a deep sense of the struggle between

[1] Perry, *The Children of the Sun.*

17

good and evil forces in the world arises in a man who must anxiously watch the seasons, and the alternations of sun and rain. Compare for instance the triumph of the Psalmist : " With His own right Hand and His holy arm hath he gotten himself the victory," and Jesus Christ forbidding Peter to strike a blow, because of a certainty of " rising again " after death, and we have a complete example of the difference between tribal and agricultural religion, the confidence of the warring nomad and the submission of the immobile tiller of the soil.

I believe that the traditional Christian attitude to matter and spirit is also traceable as much to the philosophy of growing corn as to the perplexities of sex. Here in the growth of food for men, in the changes from good years to bad, from fertility to infertility was a baffling miracle. A good spirit must be within this matter, incarnating himself, struggling with adversity that men might finally eat the body he had created. There must be some link between him and a soul or spirit in man, who likewise was struggling with adverse forces in nature and longing for the same ends—fertility, growth, prosperity. From this it is but a step to seeing in matter a prison-house and in the soul the only ultimate beauty and reality.

This attitude is something very different from that of the rational Greek to whom the struggle between mind and matter was no mystic war, but merely a question of checks and balances ; it was also very different from the attitude of a man who makes a compass of a mill wheel that he may use material forces to serve his ends. The Christian attitude to matter, it cannot be too clearly said, is one that is based upon fear, impotence, and ignorance. Had agriculture developed, as many modern industrial processes do, as an offshoot of scientific knowledge about the world, religion as we know it might never have existed.

As it was, men were pre-occupied with fertilization whether of the soil, their wives, or their animals in a mystic way because they did not understand it. They gave to pain and death a mystic significance because they saw them accompanied by creation and re-birth. Rites and taboos were wrapped about sex, marriage, and childbirth, as about the growth of the crops. Every phase of life had to be invested with sacraments expressing the struggle between the spiritual and material. Ultimately under stress of frequent disillusion and disaster, they made of birth and seasonal renewal a symbol of a life to come in which the evil forces working through matter should no longer have power to thwart the radiant purposes of the soul. Manicheism (the belief that matter is the evil principle) is twisted in and out of the fabric of Christian thought, though it is officially marked down as a heresy. It is important to get clear the religious view of matter because so much in ethical and political thought is traceable to this cause. Most modern men and women have in theory rejected asceticism. I believe, however, that many beliefs and ways of feeling still survive which were grounded in asceticism, and have no justification apart from it.

The view of the Christian ascetic was always that he could either subdue matter by his indomitable soul, scourging, starving, neglecting his body, or flee from it in visions and dreams, finally vanquishing it by an ignominious escape through the gate of death.

The idea that the glory of the soul might be apparent through the vigour and splendour of the body was sin. Every bodily process was despised. In the time they could spare from wrestling with seductive demons, the medieval mystics would sometimes describe the bodily processes which the Lord would substitute for digestion in the transmuted heavenly bodies they were to receive. The implied criticism on His present handiwork they ignored. But that criticism is not ignored by the fine lady to whom smells and child-bearing are revolting, nor by the fine gentleman who loathes hard work and despises coarse hands. Yet these are the logical consequence of Christian asceticism. If the body be believed horrible, rough toil a penance and a punishment, contemplation the supreme good, and pain the subjugation of the body to exalt the soul, then it follows as the night the day, that the conception of civilized existence will be to praise all that is artificial, to avoid loathsome work for contemplative idleness, and to neglect a diseased and dirty body on the plea that it houses a meek and pious mind. True the saints enjoin upon the Christian worldlings the right use of things material, to eat without enjoyment, to procreate without pleasure, to tend a family without delight and in a spirit of Christian authority, to see in married life duties, burdens, and consolations [1] and in the whole of existence a wearisome waiting for the longed-for release of death. No wonder many Christians meet death with fortitude, anyone might be glad to leave a world so conceived. Is it not obvious that this ascetic attitude, so far from being dignified and exalted, is mere puerile abdication? It says in effect that we should do nothing intelligent to manipulate matter, but rather endure patiently the worst that primeval chaos can do. We must live out our sixty or seventy years, mortifying the body in the sense that every instinct or desire is violated by repression and cross-examination. Love is to be " pure " and above the senses, to be robust is to be pagan.

It follows that the material expression we give to our outlook—for so long as we are in the world at all we are bound to give such

---

[1] This was put forward by an Anglo-Catholic quite recently in a letter to *The Common Cause*.

expression—will bear the mark of this struggle and suppression. There grows up an idea of civilized life on earth, as distinct from the self-mortifying existence of the saint, and the notion of this civilization will be to run right away from matter and instinct instead of permeating or cooperating with them. Thus a civilized man or woman will be one who is as far removed as possible from the tyranny of work or the life of instinct. Food, drink, clothes, habits will be designed to emphasize the triumph of that deliverance by their artificiality. Gentility will demand a life whose elegance displays its horror of utility and a refined art whose scrolls and flourishes express its divorce from practical uses. Corsets and crinolines are the logical outcome of religious civilization. They take their rise from precisely the same inspiration as Puritanism, namely, an ignorant mysticism which superimposes on instinct and matter arbitrary shapes and institutions that have no relation to any purpose whatsoever but to produce rigidity. The life of Europe up till now has been treading the path of corset civilization. Its laws and customs are guided by an *a priori* religious ethic, not by any consideration of needs and creative desires. Its ideal of beauty or perfection is something as far removed as possible from the primitive. It runs away, it suppresses, it refuses to examine, it crushes and distorts. Such a method of civilization, like the corset on the body, may for a time produce a certain rigid beauty, but predisposes to degeneracy and decay. One may read its condemnation in a thousand natural creatures and events. Watch for instance the flight of a seagull, whose perfection and beauty arise not from rigid virtue, but a perfect adaptation. Does it achieve that proud swoop, that soaring rhythm in the wind by despising its blood, bones, and feathers? How blind human civilization has been and how blind it still is, to its possibilities. We Europeans have clapped and strapped upon us this absurd Judaic-cum-Christian synthesis that is ideally adapted to produce the maximum of unhappiness. Our priests and teachers have built upon the New Testament a passive and negative morality that stifles the creative impulses, and through the Old Testament we are encouraged to set free the instincts of hatred, cruelty, and destruction. Thus our rulers can alternately hold us in patient suffering, or hurl us forth into a godly war.

An obvious correlative of a mystic horror of matter is an embargo on exact knowledge. Fear and contempt arise first of all from ignorance, and then are preserved by a deliberate refusal to know. Thus the tree of knowledge is in the Old Testament legend the source of all evil in the world, and the teachers of religion stand in the path of science at every stage of human history. When they can no longer oppose they accept new knowledge and give to it some distorted interpretation. This happened with Newton and with Darwin, and it is now happening with Einstein. The anti-evolutionists in Monkeyville, U.S.A., are right when they say that education is the enemy of ecclesiastical religion, and those who believe in human development and happiness ought to be prepared to meet them and fight upon that basis. The whole of modern history goes to show that the possession of every weapon of Church and State, the power to slay, imprison, torture, excommunicate, and suppress has not availed in the long run against the rising tide of enlightenment. Knowledge cannot fail to drive out fear and with fear will pass the chief inspiration of passive and persecuting religions. Public opinion is the source of power and no synthesis can continue to oppress when it is really no longer believed by the mass of the people. But every synthesis which has endured for long has innumerable roots and tendrils that are not always easily traceable to their source and are therefore difficult to disentangle and destroy.

Respect for authority is another principle of ecclesiastical religion and ethics. Here again the development of a supreme god drawn from sun-worship gives to Church and State the impress of autocracy. I said that the Greeks were undemocratic because they did not solve the problem of manual labour, nor apply their philosophy of life to women and the slave class. Christianity on the contrary gave to everyone the chance of a good life and of immortality. In the realm of thought this attitude was exactly reversed. Whereas to the Greek, the conduct of the individual or the community depended mainly on the conclusions reached by a group of wise men in discussion, for the Christian all rules of conduct were determined by God-given laws. Therefore, throughout our Christian communities reverence for a head authority was inculcated, first God, then the Pope, then the King, then the landlord and priest and finally the father of the family. Each of these had power to lay down rules said to be derived from God and therefore to be obeyed. Obviously, such rules, since they must be obeyed, need not consider the happiness or well-being of those on whom they were imposed, and every one of these vicars, or vicarious substitutes for God, was in a position to use his power for his own advantage. Such behaviour could easily find justification, for the more the common people suffered on earth, the greater would be their reward in the kingdom of Heaven.

Another aspect of Christian ethics which is usually praised even by non-believers, is the doctrine of charity, almsgiving, and love for one's neighbour. Interpreted as communism, such a precept might be beneficial, but not even then if it means doing such violence to egoistic impulses as to generate hatred. But in actual fact, the Churches have firmly declared themselves against such interpretations, and ranged themselves on the side of the defence of the rich man's property, coupled with condescending charity to the poor. Very recently the leading religious bodies in Germany declared it contrary to Christian doctrine to confiscate the property of the ex-Sovereign; the English prayer-book expressly repudiates communism; and, during the recent coal crisis in England, it was held by the majority of professing Christians that it was an outrage to suppose that Christianity ought to interfere in any way with the existing iron laws of economics. Such a view is probably sound; Christians must suffer evil and do individual good; large scale good and large scale evil whether here or to come are the Divine province. The poor and unfortunate are always with us; we do them good, not because it can really help them, but because it benefits our own souls and theirs. Abolish poverty and suffering? how could we dare, are they not by Divine wisdom fore-ordained?—and here lurks the old Jewish belief that men who suffer must really in some way have offended against

God's laws. Give to your neighbour of your charity, not because it is his full right to have and enjoy as much of life's delights as you yourself possess. Shall we ever rid our social philosophy of this mean and ungenerous doctrine, this charity, this philanthropy on which nearly all our social reforms have been based? It infests even socialist and Labour movements, and wherever it goes it brings psychological harm both to them that give and them that receive. With what swelling superiority the rich man drops a penny in the almsplate after a good Sunday dinner, with what swelling rage, envy, and despair the proud poor man receives the beggar's share. What expert psychologist would ever expect him to be humble and grateful, either him or the little slum boy who receives at Christmas time the broken cast-off toys generously given by little boys from the houses of the rich? We shall never be rid of it till we no longer believe this world a vale of tears ; till courage casts out fear and rights replace false senti-ment ; till we make an end of poverty ; till knowledge and science take the place of rigid dogma in the attempt to civilize our baser passions. Does it not take as many vitamins and calories to build the body of a street urchin as to build the bodies born in comfortable homes ? This truth is more palatable than charity, and will prove more powerful than philanthropy in sweeping away for ever sickness, poverty, and suffering from the world.

Many people with a reverence for traditional Christianity will cry out that this picture is distorted. Let them think again. I do not say that " true Christianity " might not be, has not often been, otherwise, though I believe that it never sufficiently escapes from its original background to avoid most of the defects described above. Nor do I say that all people within the Christian State have adhered rigidly to its doctrines. This would be difficult, for the doctrines are self-contradictory. Not all Christians, certainly, have indulged carnal desires with due sacramental reverence, and eschewed pomp and vanities for the hair shirt and the cowl, sold all they have and given to the poor. And plenty of simple people—especially women—have lived robust and beautiful and happy lives of pure instinct in the practice of Christianity at its best, imagining that the source of their activity was Christian teaching. But I maintain that I have given a just account of that structure which ecclesiastical Christianity has built in Europe, against which so many men and women of enlightenment have struggled—often in vain. It is a structure originally deriving from fear, asceticism, ignorance, and irrational, autocratic government. Of its attitude to women I have nothing to say till I come to consider their specific problems in another chapter. But I maintain in all seriousness that we cannot build an ideal of human happiness for the individual and for the community, until we have rooted out for ever the dark superstitions of the past. There is so much that is positive, glorious, inspiring, ready and waiting to be put in their place.

# II

## CONCEPTIONS OF LIFE

### MODERN RATIONALISM AND SCIENCE

The first rift in the all-enveloping cloak of the medieval synthesis was made, as everybody knows, by the return of classical learning after a thousand years of eclipse. From the taking of Constantinople by the Turks, down to our own times, Greek thought has been at its old task, leavening and civilizing the minds of European barbarians. The leaven worked slowly. The new learning was current already among the educated in France and England in the sixteenth century, but it was not until the late seventeenth and early eighteenth century that there was a powerful and abundant crop of hedonistic thought. Classical thought alone could not have made hedonism widespread or effective but for the help of science. A spreading prosperity, due to extended commerce and the discovery of new lands and new riches, also played their part in disposing people to believe that the world was not so miserable as they had thought, but it was scientific discovery that became the important basis of thinking, and of solving the practical problems of human societies. Science is really the determining factor in modern development, and the work of Galileo and Newton has more influence on the happiness and unhappiness of modern people than the teaching of Christ or the ethical precepts of Greek or Chinese philosophers. This is true as much of our theories of conduct as of the physical environment of our lives.

There are thousands of cross currents in European thought with which it is obviously not possible to deal in a short chapter, and the transition from the medieval Christian outlook to the modern has been accomplished in different countries in different ways. Spain has remained fundamentally medieval, Italy is arrested at the Renaissance, Holland, England, and Scandinavia, and Germany in the main passed through Protestantism and there also in many respects they stayed. America, taking its morals from Puritan England, shows

a similar development. France has developed
secular ethics and a secular system alongside a
disestablished but still powerful Roman church.
Thus in France, and to some extent in modern
Italy and Spain, the battle between free thought
and religion is a clearer issue than in those
countries where the half-way house of Protes-
tanism prevailed. Puritanism, which concerned
itself mainly with morals, has bitten deeper
into the conduct, though less into the minds
of its followers. Roman Catholicism, with
its insistence upon rites and dogma, has imprisoned and paralysed minds even more than
bodies. Protestants therefore tend to "virtue"
and Catholics to stupidity. Which evil is the
greater I leave my reader to decide. Spain is
a tragic example of the paralysis of mind and
will which medieval religion strictly observed
can lay upon a nation. The heretic in any age
is the seed of new life and growth. Drive him
from your borders and you will certainly
enjoy peace and quiet—the peace of stagnation
and the quiet of the grave.

Anglo-Catholics like to pretend that
Catholics are preferable to Puritans because,
though they will not let people know anything,

they at least allow them to enjoy. Historically this is quite untrue. On the contrary the Roman Church, still more than the Protestant, is bound to the asceticism of the early Fathers, and the battle which raged in eighteenth century France against traditional religion was a battle as much for happiness as for knowledge. To love and to think were the objects set forth by Voltaire as the aims of human existence, and the early theorists, previous to Voltaire, were more concerned with liberating conduct than with liberating thought. The growth of a middle class and an intelligent aristocracy and the increase of trade, had created higher standards of comfort and culture and a social ethic which was opposed, at first dumbly and unconsciously, to the rigorous asceticism of the Church. The scientific temper helped this ethic to self-analysis and expression and finally produced that rather delicious and important phenomenon the eighteenth century hedonist. It is perhaps worth while to illustrate this development from France, for there appear in clear-cut relation and sequence economics, conduct, thought and discovery working together to produce fundamental political changes. European history since the coming of science tends to belie rather than corroborate the Marxian hypothesis. Each rising class does not evolve its own philosophy, rather does it take and utilize the philosophy and discoveries of the class above, who in their turn had been shaped in conduct and manners, though not in thought, by the code of a previous generation. Thus the French aristocracy had a mode of life, which, even to its smallest detail, was influenced by the Christian synthesis, but they thought the thoughts of the Revolution. The modern middle classes in their turn, living lives which, however little they know it, are rooted in Cromwell's Puritanism or the French Revolution, are (when they think at all) thinking the thoughts which the liberated workers will utilize when they finally reach power. The reason for this lies largely in the influence of a scientific attitude to life. Science has shown men that from theory we can proceed to construction, and the practice of judging for scientific purposes helps individuals to subdue economic or instinctive prejudice.

Owing to the importance of science in daily life, this habit has spread steadily even among those who have no genuine scientific training. What is more, since the eighteenth century, a belief in human progress, however much decried, has been instinctively held by most people, and therefore each class, in so far as it thinks ahead, sows the seeds of its own overthrowing. At bottom it is foresight which has built the whole edifice of civilization and before that the nature of man himself. Our much vaunted divine nature is in its essence no more than the capacity to look a few hours, a few days, a few years, then a few centuries ahead. Other animals have not developed this faculty in like measure. And foresight has become increasingly powerful in moulding human society as the means of imparting and storing knowledge have improved. Short of a collapse and complete loss of all our present store, science will become more and more important in the theory and practice of human civilization.

Modern people, who are far removed from the bitterness of early struggles against the Christian synthesis in Europe, are too apt to accept at its face value the reading of history which Anglo-Catholicism and the Oxford movement have popularized in England. There is a tendency to minimize and brush aside the real issues and the real gains of the Reformation and the battles of eighteenth century deism. Superstitious magic has a greater hold among those who still believe in religion now than it had even sixty or seventy years ago, and here and elsewhere the pretensions of the Roman Catholics have still too great an influence even over those minds who do not accept their doctrines. The plain fact is that for a thousand years this religion of suffering interpreted by Church dignitaries and preachers maintained a hold over individual and communal life so fierce, so cruel, so intolerant that even the richest and greatest dared not call its authority in question. Knowledge was non-existent, all that makes for happiness decried. When any problem arose the Church stood, then as now, firmly on the side of the established order. No meanness, baseness, or brutality was too bad for her support. Men butchered in senseless wars, the toiling and starving masses, tortured and oppressed nations looked in vain to the sponsors of the religion of love for advocacy or deliverance. Whatever is intelligent, tolerant, loving, humane in our modern outlook came from the lips, the pens and the hearts of men and women who rejected religious dogmas and superstitious morals. The facts are there in history for all to read, and the facts of our own time bear out such a reading of history. Christian internationalism raises a timid and inconclusive head (in the absence, be it noted, of the Roman Catholics), at Stockholm in 1925, but where were these Christian hearts and voices during the years of war ? The Churches continue their policy of following and absorbing when they can no longer persecute and destroy the new morals and thought which govern successive ages.

Right on into the seventeenth century and up to the dawn of the eighteenth France remained, as is wellknown, in the grip of a medieval Church, and a temporal power which there, as in England, spoke through the divine right of kings. Church and Kings were supreme, people as little thought of openly questioning the accepted tenets of religion and morality as of flying to the moon. It would have meant contradicting the Pope, or Louis the Fourteenth, with the result in the first case of excommunication and burning, in the second the Bastille. Everything was tied up so tight, that there could be no doubt that sooner or later one of the ropes would break and everything come tumbling out in the most magnificent disorder. Which of course it did. And the rope which broke first, as I have already indicated, was that which bound people to the old ascetic ideals of conduct. Then everything followed, for let conduct once alter, and society admit the change, and many a revolutionary theory may follow. People had become rather bored with working themselves up into frenzies of fear at the terrors of hell, or ecstasies of delight in the glories of heaven : dainty meals, good plays and music, the conversation of the drawing-room, the refined love affair really seemed to them much more important. This point of view already finds expression in the plays of Molière. But as the Church went on ramping and fulminating against every little pleasure of this world, society slept more in its pew of a

Sunday, shrugged its shoulders and laughed a little and finally began to wonder if men might not walk more satisfactorily by the light of reason than they appeared to do by the light of faith. Thus the lay intellect ceased to be submissive and began openly to justify the lay mode of existence. Little books of etiquette *On Politeness, Manners, and Life*, which since the middle of the seventeenth century showed signs of the beginnings of society's self analysis now began to give way to such works as *The Art of Knowing Oneself, Happiness, Dialogues on the Pleasures, The Art of not being Bored, The Philosophy of Common Sense, The Theory of Pleasant Sensations*, and so forth. To show how ridiculous is the claim of many modern Christians that their religion has not been the enemy of the most simple pleasures of life, I will quote at length a fair sample of a dialogue on pleasure which in the year 1700 in France was suppressed and publicly burnt. It represents two men who have been to hear a sermon, walking in the garden and discussing its merits. It is called *Dialogue entre Messieurs Patru et D'Ablancourt sur les Plaisirs*, and there is nothing worse in it than the quoted passage. Both friends begin by regretting the violence of preachers, who seem to think their best qualification is good lungs and their highest eloquence achieved if they descend from the pulpit sweating from head to foot. D'Ablancourt goes on to regret the preacher's unqualified hatred of pleasure. Whatever use a man makes of pleasure, it seems he is a lost soul. " Upon my word, I am sorry that some thousand worthy folk of my acquaintance who have much virtue and yet enjoy without demur the amenities which life sometimes offers, are therefore in peril of damnation. Is there no means of procuring a little indulgence for them ? I tremble for myself at this very moment, I have just received in gift this day, two melons of fair aspect, and some admirable strawberries. That is not sinful as you know, and there is pleasure in eating them ; if then all pleasure is a crime, as your preacher assures us, I should not be very deeply grateful to that person who in sending me these fruits, either thought me wicked enough to taste of a forbidden thing, or has made me a gift which I cannot enjoy if I am a man of moral worth. And yet it would be a great pity if strawberries and melons should be forbidden in commerce. If we carry it any further, figs, grapes, and good Christian pears, won't have a better fate, and entremets and all confectioner's delights must be looked on with the same eye as arsenic. Partridges will never stand their ground against this severe morality ! I do not even know if mutton can defend itself, and you will see that in the end these devout gentlemen will reduce us to the pease-porridge of our forefathers ! "

Patru, of course, upholds the Church, but D'Ablancourt rallies him again on the utter impossibility of defending a morality which " smacks so decidedly of the deserts of Thebes ". But Patru sticks to his sturdy Cartesianism, maintaining that reason is the natural enemy of the passions, and since all pleasure means the satisfaction of the passions, then of pleasure also. So the argument goes on, D'Albancourt retorting that our senses, as well as the soul, are God-given, and should be used, but neither gentleman convinces the other. That was not to be expected.

The defenders of pleasure achieved an important victory in the capture of the highly virtuous and religious philosopher Malebranche, who saw all things in God. Malebranche, to the disgust of Arnauld the severe, and the huge joy of Pierre Bayle the free-thinker, discovered that this mortal life is after all capable of affording a man certain pleasurable sensations, and that the continuance of these sensations can even render a man happy. Malebranche was too good a psychologist to dare deny that. He admits further that the intelligent believer, for such he himself was, requires some reasonable foundation for his conduct as well as that of faith. His account of Adam before the Fall is charming. In Adam, doubtless, sense and reason did not conflict before he ate the apple, perfect harmony prevailing between all his pleasures, though he, of course, preferred those of mind and spirit to those of the body. (He does not say anything about Eve in this respect.) We heirs of the great error, however, are but too liable to prefer the pleasures of the senses—evil does not lie in them, since Adam quite obviously must have enjoyed them—it lies merely in the corruption of our will, which invests them with tyrannical power over us.

Elsewhere we find him stating that pleasure

and pain are the natural incontestable characteristics of good and evil. Providence warns us
of evil by a sensation of pain, whilst good is
accompanied by pleasurable sensations. This is
all very revolutionary for a Churchman, since
good had always been held up as a particularly
painful, but yet desirable thing in this world,
and absolutely distinct from pleasure which
was almost certainly bad. And what does the
dreadful admission about Adam having enjoyed
eating and drinking and possibly making love to
Eve (although he found the pleasures of the spirit
infinitely preferable) come to, if not that human
life *is* capable of being both good and happy ?
Thus ethics resolves itself into the regulation
and selection of the succession of joys which
shall go to its composition.

That becomes the assumption of all the
eighteenth century ethical writers, almost
without exception. Christian self-sacrifice is
seen to mean ultimate self-annihilation, and
man is regarded as a being who never had a
Fall, but in whom, as in Malebranche's Adam,
sense and reason are in perfect harmony.

The part of reason henceforth is to select
and not to domineer, our theorists concern

themselves continually with the kinds of pleasure in which an intelligent man may indulge, and it becomes evident to the reader that the degree of virtue is entirely a matter of the degree of refinement brought to life ; civilization becomes thus the touchstone of morality, and we are really back at the golden mean.

One of the most tragic figures of this period is Pascal, a man of brilliant scientific genius with an eager thirst for intellectual discovery, caught in the toils of a religion that denied all knowledge and delight, and led to mortify in the cells of Port Royal not only his pride of intellect, but all the gentle impulses of his human affections. In his tormented mind and body the two epochs clash in an agonizing battle, and he, who should have been pioneer and leader of the great company of the lovers of science and mankind, remains as their awful warning, a butt for the jests and bitter attacks of those whose temperament and period endowed them with greater courage than he possessed. " I," cried Voltaire, leading the attack, " dare to take the part of humanity against this sublime misanthropist."

" If there is a God," wrote Pascal, " we must love Him and not his creatures." On the contrary, cries Voltaire, we must love and that very tenderly, human creatures, we must love our country, wife, father, children, so much so that God makes us love them in spite of ourselves. The opposite principle makes inhuman thinkers, so much so that Pascal . . . treated his sister harshly . . . for fear of appearing to love a human creature . . . if we ought to act so, what would become of human society ? "

Or again, Pascal complains of the natural injustice of man. " Each makes for his own interest, this is contrary to social order. We must make for the general good and the tendency towards our own interest is the beginning of all disorder in war, police economics. . . ." " This is quite comformable to order," is the blunt reply. " It is as impossible to form and maintain a society without self interest as it would be to make children without concupiscence, or think of feeding oneself without appetite." It is in fact mutual need and self-interest which have led man to form society, it is our own needs which make us considerate of the needs of others. It is true that God might have created purely altruistic creatures, in which case merchants would go to India out of charity and the mason work his stone to give pleasure to his neighbours. But we are otherwise constructed, therefore let us not question our instincts but employ them.

There we have in a nutshell the eighteenth century faith in man, profoundly idealistic, and yet carrying as ballast an almost cynical and yet respectful regard for the material and petty motives which move him. But long before Voltaire penned those lines—before indeed the spirit of his age enabled him to pen them, clique and salon had been discussing virtue, pleasure, friendship, and happiness, almost always with hedonistic tendency, progressing later from these mild beginnings to the more abstruse problems of metaphysics and science.

Chief among these treatises is Fontenelle's *Thoughts on Happiness* in which is described a certain *piano* sequence of pleasures that maintain a man in a state of gentle contentment which he does not desire to change. This little treatise, slight as it is, strikes the keynote

for all subsequent ethical studies, right up
to and even past the middle of the century.
Whatever the form and argument of these
latter works, whether they are religious or
agnostic, idealistic or materialistic, whether
they inquire into the springs of human action,
or skate delicately on the surface like Fontenelle
himself, whether they deal with the individual
only or with society, one and all agree that the
goal of human nature and of the moralist is
not virtue but happiness. The degree and
nature of this happiness and its causes vary
from writer to writer, according as we are
dealing with good Christian divine, well-bred
man, libertine, or medical practitioner. Ethics
like religion is to be put on a reasonable basis,
and each man to interpret the oracle as best
he may.

Of the same date as Fontenelle's treatise
probably, is a short *Dialogue between Agathon
and Aspasia on Pleasure*, by Remond le Grec.
This is a thought more indulgent than
Fontenelle's and is interesting also, in that it
introduces aesthetic grounds for conduct.
A set of young people of both sexes are
in the country in fair weather (all the

treatises have their little setting or dedication, you can imagine the scene, the long alley-ways, the conventionally laid out gardens, the statues and fountains and ornamental waters, the exquisite pink and white ladies), and they begin to draw distinctions between delicate and coarse pleasures. The philosopher Anaxagoras, says Aspasia, maintains that some men have in them more of that celestial fire that Love breathed into the world at the Creation, and therefore seek pleasure more heartily. But objects Agathon, Socrates looks on excessive pleasure as the source of all evil. Admittedly says Aspasia, pleasure must be controlled, but it is just by their delicacy in this respect that one may recognize men of breeding. In learning, is not the discovery of a truth an intoxication of the understanding, and poetry, painting, music, the intoxication of the imagination ? Our attitude to the ordinary delights of life, good food, good wine, etc., should be aesthetic, affording us the free pleasure that art can give and not enslaving the mind.

Agathon is completely convinced, leaves for ever the ranks of the " austere " philosophers, and rather meanly hits back at them, by insinuating that they too probably believe more in Aspasia's point of view than they would care to admit.

This aesthetic attitude is to be found again in Crousaz *Of the Education of Children*, in which he suggests that a child be taught to perform certain acts, because they are beautiful rather than because they are good, and yet again in Dubos' *Reflexions on Poetry and Painting*. Dubos further defends pleasure as a perfectly natural result of a need in human beings, and boldly asserts that the pleasure afforded by art is the result of stirring the passions. But, he contends, it is better to have the emotions stirred at the risk of indulging in them too freely, than to live a life of utter boredom, which is the alternative. An austere community, from which artists were excluded, such as that foreshadowed by Plato, would be unutterably dull.

The little volume by Deslandes, *The Art of not being bored*, adopts the same outlook, though with far less psychological insight and seriousness of purpose. Deslandes is frankly a voluptuary, although an intelligent one. The art of happiness to him means the art of not being bored, and the art of not being bored the art of feeling, or skilful seeking of pleasurable sensations. This he repeats through chapter after chapter of would-be smart chit-chat, occasionally saying some very good things. He is writing his book to cheer and console a charming lady who is languishing in boredom, immured in the country with a dull husband. Whether the invitation to seek pleasurable emotion is a hint to transfer her affections to the author, I must leave the reader to judge. The pursuit of learning, to his credit be it said, is for Deslandes the next best way to avoid boredom. None the less, he deplores the remoteness and " gaucherie " of many savants and would have subscribed to the statement of Claville, a fellow hedonist of later date, who says, " We must know, but above all, we must know how to live." Though the man of learning was infinitely preferable in their view to the vulgar commercial who amassed riches, yet both gave first place to the cultured individual of moderate means who knew how to enjoy life. Deslandes was himself a passable philosopher and a man of science, and as such, knew what intellectual joys could mean, but apparently, all things considered, he gives his vote to the joys of emotion. He envies women their delicious preoccupation with their emotions, the finest recipe for the avoidance of boredom. Elsewhere he exclaims : " Man is unhappy only because he thinks, and he thinks as much from pride as from necessity. That is the sum total of our mistakes . . . our thoughts destroy us." Nature is kind only to those who enjoy, and do not seek to probe her mysteries, and thus we should live by our natural instincts, among which apparently the need for thought is not counted. " Though I shock the most superb of prejudices I maintain that reason is drab and useless when it seeks to place us above everything by the power of thought." But Deslandes is nothing if not inconsistent, for barely two pages further on he assures us that " to feel properly we must cast aside all the passions that proceed from nature and make others according to their pattern, which shall be less violent."

It goes without saying that the authors of all these studies in hedonism are men of solid social and financial position. How many men can sit down to write a eulogy of sweet content, who are not blest with a sufficiency, or even an abundance, of this world's goods. For " humble happiness " we must here read not the true philosopher's crust of bread and pitcher of water, but good cheer, delicate meats, clothes and company, and for " obscure happiness " not the nameless hovel, but a well-appointed mansion, frequented by a large circle of influential and flattering friends. In this state of " humble and obscure happiness " many a " philosopher " lived to a ripe and rotund old age. Fontenelle, indeed, pursuing his policy of refined selfishness in every detail, attained his century of years. But to do them justice, these very accommodating and unheroic moralists are sound and unflinching in their opposition to that hectic " getting and spending " and " laying waste of powers " which ever prevails in the world at large. They preach study, peace, gentleness, tolerance, the academic and contemplative ideal, never fully enough understood or practised at any period of the world's history, and yet rich with a thousand graces and delights. It would be pure folly to attempt to comfort the man who barely survives in the struggle for existence with such ethical systems as these, but what better maxims could be put before those in easy circumstances, than to avoid ostentation, display, and excess, and to devote their leisure and substance to art and learning and the cultivation of grace and beauty in every form ? And it was to such as these that our philosophers dedicated their little brown volumes. We may blame them for their lack of understanding of the grim reverse of the picture—the "tiers etat", but, none the less, it was their gentle Epicureanism that, by fostering benevolence and tolerance, in time brought to birth those ideals of humanitarianism and social revolution whose vast potentiality mankind is not even yet in a position to estimate.

It is an amazing and glorious spectacle to see unfolding as the century unfolds, all the flowers of thought, all the spreading trees of social and political reform, that sprang from that one seed, the little statement " Man has a right to be self-interest, man has a right to be happy". Turning uneasily in her slumber, seventeenth century France murmured it, and it became a flame, and then a consuming fire, fierce in destruction, that transformed first the face of France herself, and then leapt forth to kindle the world.

For there can be little doubt that the ideals of human brotherhood and democracy which ultimately brought about the Revolution, and which are moving humanity so profoundly to-day, had their roots in the theories of the early eighteenth century hedonists ; and they again owed everything to the gentleman who so resolutely refused to be damned for eating strawberries and melons. The cloud no bigger than a man's hand is herald of a deluge ; from such concealed and negligible sources do the relentless streams of progress rise.

So far, it is obvious, all these people are mainly talking about the old golden mean, and trying to set out its boundaries, and the confusion of mind we have just analysed in Deslandes, indicates that there is already very grave difficulty among the hedonists on just this point. Granted that pleasure corresponds to a definite need in mankind, and that the search for it is a natural instinct, exactly how far *is* it to be indulged ? They can give no conclusive answer. All they can say is " Follow the light of nature ", and " There are some pleasures that are higher than others, good taste will teach you which ". Fontenelle counsels the avoidance of violent delights, and the cultivation of the quiet life. Desfourneaux, another theorist who has not yet been mentioned, agrees, quibbling, however, a little over the first premiss, by insisting that men do *not* seek happiness but rather riches, power, and position, and need to be enlightened as to what really brings content. Yet a third Dupuy, in a set of dialogues addressed to a young man entering on the world and exposed to its temptations, with what a Jesuit reviewer calls " A morality at once commonsensical and sublime " gives as a motto : " The great art of being happy in life is to abstain from pleasure when the necessity ceases." Then we have the aesthetes. And lastly, Deslandes, who *wants* to put no check on nature, and yet feels that he must, his scientific studies teaching him that besides being quite unmoral, nature is entirely unrestrained. One more step and we shall reach naturalism.

In a very brief but refreshingly clear analysis of the nature of pleasure and pain, in which he comes to the conclusion that pain predominates in the world, Maupertuis makes the bold assertion that higher and lower pleasures do not exist, and that the only criterion of pleasure is its intensity or duration. Philosophers have always emphasized too greatly either physical or mental pleasure, this being very largely the difference between Epicurean and Stoic, but really all pleasures are of the soul, whether they come through the bodily organs or no. " Let us not fear to compare pleasures of the senses with the most intellectual pleasures, let us not cherish the illusion that there are some pleasures more noble than others ; the most noble pleasures are those which are greatest." This statement, completely logical as it is, was very severely criticized on account of its possible implications. For the Epicureans had been glad to safeguard themselves by the intellectual, refined, aesthetic quality of their pleasures, but if all pleasure were to be accounted the same ultimately ? Like Deslandes, Maupertuis stopped short. But Lamettrie, a doctor, completely immersed in the study of anatomy, and not endowed with a great deal of aesthetic or intellectual refinement, boldly went forward, and in *Man a Machine*, stated the case for nature and naturalism without humbug, ascribed his book to the far more cautious and delicate Marquis d'Argens, and flung it on the world, heartily enjoying the scandal it provoked. In it he maintains that the scientist and physician know more about the " labyrinth of man " than divines and moralists, with their " dark and idle studies ", pleads for the scientific method in all branches of study, especially ethics, insists that the human mind changes with the variations of the human body—men of valour are those who eat heartily—thus really reversing Maupertuis' point that all sensations are of the mind because ultimately felt there. They are of the body, says Lamettrie, for thence they start. The influence of scientific study is here paramount, though even Deslandes had dared to say that he would advise the melancholy man to seek advice not from priest or moralist, but from the doctor. Lamettrie's views on happiness are such as might be expected from so frank a materialist. There is no juggling with delicacy, high and low pleasures, good taste. There is only one life and one happiness, and that here and now; and happiness is love of life. The happiest man is he who is most gifted. Where nature has not endowed a man so completely he can do much to improve himself and so have a greater capacity for happiness, but *natural* happiness, not the conventional kind taught us by education. Man should even do things which cause him remorse and get over a feeling so childish, only planted in him by environment and education. Nature is to be followed, and she is self-sufficient. If men were only brave enough they would admit that so-called virtue is but a social and relative conception, those who live by it have a certain happiness because they like it, and moreover, they have their reward in the esteem of their fellow men. For this social virtue is like an old hag with a diamond ring on her finger, her wooers love her only because they covet the diamond. Those who do not serve humanity have their own kind of happiness, too, nature sees to that, since she is self-sufficient, and despises any attempt to graft a system of ethics upon her. By this self sufficiency of nature it would seem that Lamettrie means that every man has a right to his own ethical standards, which is about as revolutionary a doctrine as could be imagined, and involves the complete destruction of ethics. But this position is quite a logical development from that of his predecessors. Losing religion as a basis and sanction for morality, they had said : " Nature is both good and happy, follow her." What Lamettrie says in effect is : " I know nature to be happy, I don't know whether she is good or bad, it doesn't seem to me to matter, follow her just the same."

There are but two more hedonists of whom I should like to speak. Both of them show in somewhat similar ways, as Deslandes and Lamettrie also show, the modifications which natural science begins to introduce into the old systems drawn from the Classics. Louis de la Caze, a doctor like Lamettrie and also predominantly interested in anatomy, maintains in a series of interminable dialogues between a physician and a moralist, that the whole happiness of man depends upon the depression and release of his diaphragm! Happiness, to him, is a sense of security, attained by primitive man apparently, by the immediate destruction of what he feared, whether an enemy or a beast of prey. Fear is thus the first unpleasing emotion to dispose of, if we want happiness, for fear more than anything causes the diaphragm to contract, so interrupting the action of the bodily organs. In primitive life the possibility of acting promptly to stave off a menace, re-establishes physical harmony, and so happiness. But this is not so easy in civilized life, where a man is constantly assailed by little cares and fears, against which he cannot take immediate and bold action, with the sad result that his diaphragm remains semi-contracted, and this upsets his digestion and renders him uneasy and miserable. We must, therefore, take care to provide in civilized life, by means of art and science, and other interesting occupations, an outlet for the suppressed natural instincts and passions which would have found freer and fuller play in a more primitive state. This sounds rather like Freud, who does, in fact, in many respects resemble de la Caze.

Here is a passage from de la Caze, which might have come from Freud's book on *Wit*, so devoid is it of that quality. " A general who wins a battle, a woman who enjoys the triumph of her charms, an author who sees his fame growing, what do they feel in these agreeable moments ?   At bottom it is simply strong vibrations favourable to the play of the diaphragm."

We cannot dally longer with de la Caze, though he has a great deal more to say, some of it quite wise, but most of it such as we have already found elsewhere.  For the last hedonist, we have to go back a little—to the seventeen thirties—for de la Caze is past the mid-century.

Levesque de Pouilly's treatise on the *Theory of Pleasant Sensations*, the outcome of a bet made with Lord Bolingbroke after an argument between them, is one of the earlier ones in which science is genuinely and intelligently applied to explain and assist happiness.

To him all happiness consists in the healthy state and healthy exercise of all faculties of mind and body, so as neither to tire nor under-develop them.   Children delight in play, young people in dancing and hunting, not because—as Pascal has it—of their innate frivolity, but because the exercise is necessary to their bodies, driving away vapours and humours through perspiration. (He is relying on the experiments of a seventeenth century Italian physician, Sanctorius.) Again he instances the pleasure of the eye in contemplating certain colours, and quotes Newton's Optics to demonstrate that those which are fatiguing—such as orange and red, cause too great vibration of the nerves, while those which we consider dull, such as grey and brown, do not cause them to vibrate sufficiently. The pleasure of music, again, is due to the way in which the nerves of the ear respond to sound— discords jangling and hurting them. He goes on to deal with mental pleasure, which, again, is due primarily to the exercise of the brain matter, and he hazards the suggestion, that the more delicate the mental organs, the subtler the forms of intellectual exercise in which a man delights. As to pleasures of the heart, all emotions of a certain degree of violence, except fear or hatred, are pleasant—and this involves him in an interesting discussion of the pleasure evoked by tragedy and other forms of art. Difference in tastes Pouilly ascribes entirely to difference in strength and size of the physical organs—a man with strong optical nerves would tend to delight in bright colours, and so on. God is dragged in at the tail end of the work, as the author and designer of our physical and mental organization and as such to be obeyed and worshipped.

The most famous, but by no means the most extreme or logical, of the defenders of nature is Jean Jacques Rousseau. Lamettrie and others did arrive at the position that the natural and instinctive life of man might be ethically neutral. Rousseau, however, steadily maintained that the source of human corruption was civilization and the towns and that men and women at work in the countryside, loving one another and their offspring in strict monogamy, were naturally virtuous. Rousseau's theory of human nature was pleasantly flattering and therefore widely believed. It was the chief basis of the French Revolution and its influence echoes and re-echoes in our education, our political and social life. Riotous individualism, self-expression, yielding to impulse, the simple life are all characteristics of Rousseauism in modern thought, and all of us to-day go far beyond what Rousseau wrote in our assertions of personal character and freedom. A distinguishing mark of Rousseau as compared with other theorists of his century was his emphasis on the dignity of simple manual work, and the working classes. There is very little about the pleasure of work—other than intellectual—in the upper class hedonists, for they were removed from economic necessity. To the eighteenth century religious preachers also, work is still a duty laid upon man by God. Voltaire championed the rights of man in general and was good to his dependents and poorer neighbours, but he did not incite a peasant revolt. He fought the arbitrary power of Church and King over men's souls and bodies, but he did not idolize work or the character of common men.

In Jeremy Bentham, who represents in England the culmination of a development similar to that described in France, the importance of the masses of common people comes out in the theory of the " greatest happiness of the greatest number". Like the other theorists Bentham analyses the impulses of man and their individual and social expression, and from his analysis moves forward to create a political philosophy. The creation of such a philosophy had very soon become a conscious aim. It was thought that men could have natural religion apart from dogma and superstition, and that the principles of morals could be established on an exact scientific basis like mathematics. From a close study of the nature of man, without Christian bias, the theorist was to proceed to the rules which ought to govern human society. Man left alone, without companions, might do anything he chose: rules, however, must be accepted in a community. But if such rules enjoined merely the abstract principles of self-denial and virtue, clearly anything might be demanded of the citizens by the holders of power. Therefore the basis of society must be the right of the common or garden human being to happiness. This is an assertion of first-rate importance. The endless discussions to which it leads on high and low pleasures, reason and the passions, the goodness or badness of " nature " do not display the confusion of wickedness astray from the laws of

God. On the contrary, they are the genuine attempts of men to read their own thoughts and feelings by the light of science rather than mystic prejudice. What is man? Must he be crushed to virtue? Can we not live at peace one with another? These were the questions the eighteenth century asked, to which subsequent generations are seeking to return an answer. The search for a science of morals, and so of politics, though it cannot be pursued as exactly as the eighteenth century supposed, does not therefore stand condemned as vain and fruitless. Very much has already been achieved. We have been influenced in judgments of every degree of importance by their ethical method. None but bigoted Christians in the modern world decide ethical questions by a simple reference to Divine Laws. We ask ourselves, not, " Is this the commandment of God ? " but " Does this action bring harm or pain to myself or to other human beings ? " By this standard many things not condemned in the Ten Commandments or Christian teaching are seen to be harmful, and many things that are there forbidden not only harmless but beneficial.

Two things, however, confuse the minds of the eighteenth century hedonists. One is the dualism of mind and matter inherited from asceticism, and the other the mechanical nature of science as they understood it. Reason governing the passions, mind controlling matter were but another expression of the Christian spirit taming the unruly flesh. Cartesianism, Calvinism, Puritanism, all of these were at bottom still propounding medieval psychology. Whether it were reason, moral force, or the soul of man, there was still according to these doctrines a faculty which held in check man's animal nature. Thorough going materialists, on the other hand, were governed by mechanics in their theory of the human mind and body. They did not know what chemistry, biology, and psychology have since taught about the complexity of our structure. They thought of a human being as a watch wound up, or a bundle of bones held together and propelled about by the mechanical movements of the muscles. Similarly society and the universe was a whirl of matter in motion, governed, some said by chance, others by the Divine intelligence. Therefore, though the instincts of human beings were analysed and lay bare before their eyes, traditional psychology and the influence of mechanism prevented men from really understanding the meaning of the analysis themselves had made.

Instead of treating each man as a haphazard bundle of instincts the deep flow and satisfaction of which might bring him happiness, they took him to be a rational being, composed of mind and passions, a body ruled and moved by an intelligent soul. They did not say simply a man desires food, sex, children, these can make him happy ; they said he is a rational being pursuing pleasure and pleasure makes him happy, which is quite a different thing. Despite Voltaire's denial of the possibility, there were in his period men still sufficiently dominated by asceticism as to believe that a man could eat and marry and care for children from pure reason rather than instinct, and that this fact constituted him a nobler being than an animal. This excessive rationalizing of instinct and insistence on human dignity lead to the whole pleasure-pain psychology. Man had so long been regarded as the chosen of God, fallen from his high estate, that he could not bring himself to recognize complete kinship with animals. Animals might be driven purely by instinct to grasp this or that object, but the dignity of man required that, if he no longer sought virtue, he should at least consciously and intelligently seek pleasure. He must hold on to his ego, formerly his immortal soul, he could not become a blind thing driven hither and thither by impulse. I believe this pleasure psychology to be as mistaken as the theory of moral virtue, and for similar reasons. It involves us in an absurd and unnecessary dualism, and leads to the endless squabbles about high and low pleasure, and the difference between pleasures of the moment and abiding contentment. Happiness has very little to do with immediate sensations of pain and pleasure, and if we are guided solely by rational choice we shall almost certainly miss what most we need in life. Instinctive happiness is frequently accompanied by responsibility, anxiety, and pain. It is not bought by sacrifice, but neither is it won by sipping and measuring and counting of the cost.

The less we indulge in high falutin' bombast

and false pride the nearer do we come to a solution of individual and social problems. To find out every important need of human nature and to satisfy it, without regard to aesthetic or moral judgments that have no relation to the happiness of other human beings, should be the function of the practical politician. Some men and women may guide their individual lives by judgments which to them have an aesthetic or moral value, but they are not thereby nobler than the simplest of instinctive creatures. The manipulation and guidance of instinct is discussed in later chapters, but here it is enough to say that reason as conqueror or charioteer of unruly passions is, though an improvement on asceticism pure and simple, not a final solution of the problem of civilization.

From the rational search for pleasure derives a great deal that is limited and superficial in modern thought. It is undeniable that the development of foresight has gradually built up in us the habit of weighing up future pleasure against present pain, or present pleasure against future pain, and that in this way we can make for ourselves a selective philosophy of life. But to imagine that everybody does this, or ought to do this, is a mistake. It is also a mistake to think that this is a base description of man's nature. On the contrary, if everybody were moved by rational hedonism the world might be a better place than it is. It is because people are not that we have wars and oppressions. It is also because they are not that some of them know the deepest joys of love and creation. It may be true that a man will sacrifice thousands of lives sooner than give up sixpence of his income, but it is also true that when he is angry he will fling away a fortune to injure another individual or a nation. Even anger is not needed, men do this deliberately for the sake of a traditional class prejudice or a worn out superstition. The pleasure-pain psychology and scientific mechanism (not science) underlie the theories of very many modern thinkers. Enlightened self interest is taken by them to mean that the average man is moved by economic motives in all his actions and thoughts. The " natural " laws which the eighteenth century sought are held to be economic laws which are cast iron and incapable of change. They govern wages, they determine minds. In the back of men's minds the notion is born that if these laws can be discovered they can be set free to govern society.[1] There are two versions of this theory, one the familiar capitalist argument for unrestricted competition in buying and selling and employing, the other the half-truth of Marxist economic determinism in history. The Marxist is a very special kind of materialist, for he holds that character and beliefs are not physically and materially, but economically determined. He visualizes a society in which rational men at the centre of things offer organization and economic security to a mass of " economic men " who accept these benefits in return for their labours.

Such a society resembles the Newtonian universe, and the people in it, like planets or lumps of matter pushing to their own selfish ends, are held together by reason as the universe is by the force of gravitation. Even so, such a picture of society is an advance on the annihilation of every impulse to happiness

[1] Clearly this is false reasoning, because if there are certain unchangeable laws, they operate already and the present state of our lives results from them. The fact that the state of society changes so much proves that the laws are easily broken, therefore hardly immutable.

in the service of God-given kings and laws. It admits that a scheme of society must have some regard, though very slight, to the needs of the individuals that compose it. No one seems to have noticed that some of the most important things in human life are left out of this system. Things that should be deep and fundamental are left to hang upon it like ivy clinging to an unyielding wall. But, like the ivy, these things have a way of chipping cracks in the smoothest surfaces. I mean sex love and love of children. Wife and family that had been a part of life hang on the " economic man " as an excrescence or a luxury. There is no room for them in the scheme of things. Sometimes one is tempted to wonder if the whole course of thought and of history might not have been changed, had women achieved political rights at the same time as the bulk of men. Large scale organization saw them driven back from co-operation with men in work to become more and more dependent upon masculine bounty. Traditionally regarded as less rational and more instinctive than men, they were not included in the category of enlightened self-interest and were left to minister, against fearful odds, to all those needs and desires which men failed to satisfy in their rational society.[1]  Emerging, they were still so bewildered by masculine prestige as to accept at face value man's theories.  There were able women in the eighteenth century, but they did not struggle for feminine emancipation.[2]  There were able women in the nineteenth, but they wanted to make women the copies of men.  Only to-day do we find women challenging in word or deed asceticism, dualism, mechanism, and the " economic man " in favour of a society built direct upon instinctive needs, on all, not only one, of the profound desires of human nature.

Eighteenth century dualism of mind and matter does ultimately derive from medieval asceticism, but there are important differences.

[1] It is not only the lack of votes, but the loss of their important functions in home industries which has enslaved women.  Where, as in Lancashire, they work as well as keep home and children, the results of slavery to economics and mechanism are terrible to contemplate.  The mill governs all : falling in love, having children, are inconvenient weaknesses of animal nature.  This attitude has ground its way into the characters of the people themselves.

[2] With the one glowing exception of Mary Wollestone-craft.

If there still remains the notion of the mind in control of the " lower " nature there is not the same horror and suspicion of matter as characterizes the religious outlook. Matter may be moved, manipulated and understood by mind. There is mechanical invention, there is even the probability that human nature can be changed for the better. Here, again, the analogy with mechanical invention has misled eighteenth century and modern thinkers as to the speed and manner of human progress. It was, and is still, widely held that reason, making a sudden change, can, through economic laws and propaganda, immediately change human nature. Men can be brought to see the folly of war and will then abandon it, they can be made economically secure and will then go forward in co-operation in place of deadly rivalry. All this is not false, but it is only half the truth. It does not go deep enough into human psychology.

Certainly an appeal to reason has more power over men economically secure, than over the baulked and starving, but the appeal to unreason remains potent. This is not because of the inherent wickedness of man, as the theologian pretends, but because heredity, habit, starved desires, false religions twist their strong tendrils around the limbs that struggle for freedom. We cannot treat each individual as a unit, a new creation, body and soul, or reason and passions, nor can we treat him as purely determined by economics. Human progress is real, but slow, complex, involving millions of factors which must be studied. It is not to be dealt with by cheap and superficial psychology, sudden conversions, sudden mechanical constructions such as the Christian, the pure rationalist and the Marxist can offer. But it does not follow that we cannot deal with it at all.

The emotional current set flowing by Rousseau was the obvious counterpart to intellectual hedonism. Rousseau stated the case for an instinctive life, but the price he demanded was the destruction of any complex or highly organized society. This error has been repeated by many other reformers— Tolstoy, for example, in his return to the peasant life and Gandhi with his spinning wheel. And Rousseau was not really honest about nature. He depicts love and parental feeling with the unctuous sentimentality of a mere spectator, for a man may remain so even after the experience. In spite of his emphasis on " natural " goodness, it is by religion and stoic virtue that his admired characters are maintained. A return to nature can obviously be only a matter of degree, even Rousseau never advised sacrificing the arts of agriculture and adopting the life of the noble savage pure and simple. What Rousseau chief among others really did was to uphold animal life in an age which, from traditional asceticism and present rationalism, no longer understood its real meaning. Bodily delights had been freely spoken of, but the bodily health and beauty which can come of simple feeding, exercise, fresh air, were little understood. These are commonplaces to us now, in our enjoyment and vocabulary, and so is the beauty of hill, valley, woodland, and sea. It is Rousseau who restored these things, and the importance of their restoration[1] is enormous. Thus, in a sense, Rousseau stands for the country; rationalism

[1] It may be argued that the nature cult is an example of high civilization. The savage did not enjoy nature in any conscious artistic way.

and the ascetic for the towns. It is interesting to notice in consequence that the back to nature cult has gone on from Rousseau's time to our own, for the most part distinct and separate from the theories based upon reason, economics and science. The cult of instinct has nearly always been anti-social, undisciplined, barbaric, and leading to chaos. Nobody ever dreamt it could be anything else because they thought of instinct as a raw and savage impulse that could only be checked or destroyed but never modified. Thus the believers in instinct have never been politically effective save as a bulwark to a stolid conservatism. The struggle for reform was left to economics, to rationalism, and to a thin and watery humanitarianism. All this is a part of the price we have paid for the leadership of ascetics and puritans. But for their teaching we might long since have understood and ministered to the use of instinct in a complicated and civilized society. In the advocacy of instinct no less than in the appeal to reason a historical perspective is necessary. Use and disuse of faculties, acquired knowledge, the exercise of the imagination all play their part in influencing the flow and expression of instinct. We have to go deeper than economics, deeper than psychology and medicine, back into race and heredity, the chemistry of organic and plant life, into physics and the nature of the universe. This has occupied the scientists while politicians and moralists were still raving.

The nineteenth century has seen the working out in our social system of the dry and mechanical picture of the world, which resulted from imposing on human nature shaped by ascetic religion the early mechanical theories of economics and science. Any scientific theory that is treated as dogma and unrelated to other branches of science can become a tyranny like a religion. It can have even more power than religion over the destiny and happiness of men and women, because it does not only hold their imaginations and minds, but can be used to alter every detail of their environment. Thus industrialism has realized eighteenth century discoveries in the practical material world and had far-reaching effects upon our habits and character. Following on our usual human method of trial and error, the only way in which we ever make real changes, we now come to see the limitations and dangers of the system we have created. We blame science or the capitalists for our discomforts and misfortunes. But merely to blame and destroy will carry us nowhere. Stupid rich men and our own limited knowledge are undoubtedly at fault ; but if we had not first built the system we could not know either its magnificent possibilities or its terrible dangers. We must find out what is wrong and put it right, not waste our time in sentimental regrets or passionate and angry blaspheming. One thing which is seriously wrong is our age-long neglect of the roots of primitive feeling. We concentrated first on the soul, then the mind, to the neglect of the sources of emotion. We were so dazed by industrialism and the towns that we forgot their essential adjuncts, agriculture and the country. Many people all through the nineteenth century were worried by what was happening. They felt the need of emotional expression and found no simple and direct ways of expressing it in their individual lives or the structure of society. Trade went well for the most part, prosperity grew, but still people felt an emotional hunger, which grew more intense and widespread until it broke out in the cataclysm of the European war. People lamented that love of beauty was passing with the passing of handicrafts, that industrialism was making an ugly wilderness of the world. Sex love and love of children were denied and thwarted in ways we shall later discuss. All of this has been diagnosed by the Churches as hunger for God and the things of the spirit. Therefore, beside the artists who tried to restore handicrafts, the romantics who sought in medieval castles and mysteries a glamour and beauty which they felt were departing from their age, we have the cult of Merrie England and the Oxford movement. All of it no more than an offshoot of Rousseauism, dreams and vain sighings for a world long since gone by, the day dreams of men and women who could not face reality or adjust themselves to master their new environment. All this emotional unrest is no awful nemesis on impious materialism, on the contrary it is a sign that the study of things material has not gone far or deep enough. It is the logical result of misreading matter and seeing in instinct something necessarily anti-social and barbarous. The brilliant and broidered cloak of medieval superstition, the chasubles, the banners and the blessings, the quiet backwaters where men lie drowsing over the past, are but an abdication and a bankruptcy. Love of beauty, love of mate and children, discovery, adventure, courage, must speak through our own realities, the technique, the knowledge, and the mechanism of our own time. If we are not equal to this task then these deep wells must perish, but with them will perish also our survival and our civilization.

Before I pass on to say something of the later influences of science, we may sum up briefly what modern Europe till the end of the eighteenth century had contributed to solving our problem. It defied the Church in order to reassert the principles of Greek hedonism and men's right to happiness. By defending discussion against authority and man against systems and oppressors, it laid the foundations of modern democracy. It made the first scientific discoveries which were to lead to those processes and methods which could lessen work and rescue the overburdened worker. It made the first attempts at a scientific study of human nature and morals, and sketched a theory of progress in place of individual immortality. It did next to nothing about the problems of women and children, if anything it left women worse off than before.

Goethe's *Faust* is perhaps the most significant summary of eighteenth century hopes and beliefs. Faust studies scholastic theology and dabbles into the rudiments of science. He longs for happiness and sells his soul to the devil to obtain it. He tries love, but with a woman who—whatever her charm as a poetic figure—is as antiquated a mental, moral and physical being as the wit of man could have devised. Love between the knowledge seeking, soul tormented ascetic Faust and the ignorant, pious and equally ascetic Gretchen fails as a source of happiness. It obviously would. He abandons her and their illegitimate child.

Faust follows many adventures, and finally sets to work on vast schemes of land reclamation. He does not dig himself—no—his master-mind directs others to feats of engineering. In this moment, contemplating the glory of intelligent work and the happiness which such work will bring to common simple people, Faust cries out that he is happy and the devil takes his soul. He is redeemed for his ceaseless striving, and as he is finally borne to Heaven, he visualizes the sweet soul of Gretchen whom he has abandoned to death and despair, interceding and drawing him upwards to Heaven.

In all this it is the picture of the relations of men and women that strikes most oddly upon modern minds. Man the ruthless conqueror, leaving woman that he may pursue the nobler paths of knowledge and high virtue, woman the gentle, timorous, holy, drawing her tyrant to Heaven over her mangled body by her ethereal piety and prayers.[1]

Whatever the nineteenth century did in economic structure, it gave in thought two things of first class importance—the theory of the evolution of man and the emancipation of woman. There was a widening and deepening of the application of science in all branches. The origin of species, the descent of man

[1] Cf. also Goethe's *Tasso* :—

" Willst Du genau erfahren was sich ziemt,
So frage nur bei edlen Frauen an,
Denn ihnen ist an meisten dran gelegen
Dass alles wohl sich zieme, was geschieht."

brought at last an intelligible explanation of the oddities of human nature. Until lately it seemed that we had almost recovered from our first horror at the discovery of such kinship with the lower orders of creation. But apparently there are still found men who like to despise their humble origin just as there are aristocrats who like to go on believing that their blood is blue and not red like any common man's. Evolution threw into prominence those very factors which had been formerly ignored— geography, race, heredity, the slowness of change and adaptation. It drew the attention of thinkers away from human morals, reason, and economics to seek the answer to man's riddles in the chemistry of organic matter and of the inorganic matter upon which it fed. It upheld the instincts as the primary motives of all action and development, at bottom the sources of the very reason and soul of which men had boasted so long. In evolutionary theory a human being was seen to be conditioned not only by his immediate environment, habits, and parents, but by the influence of a long line of ancestors and environments in the past. If you wanted to create a happy society therefore, you could not simply appeal to virtue or to reason, you must deal in ways that might be slow and elaborate with instincts whose past uses had perhaps been anything but generous or constructive. This study of organic life in the place of mechanism has brought many advances in medicine and surgery, and in the care and nurture of children. It has so far led to no fundamental political changes, for politicians, notoriously the most backward of the community, can still not get beyond the Middle Ages or the eighteenth century. One may say, perhaps, that the base cult of nationalism and of herd instinct is the politician's version of the struggle for existence, he has used the same theory to reinforce the fierceness of economic competition. That it is possible, having discovered a struggle for existence, to set to work to mitigate or eliminate it; or, having found some herd co-operation among men, to turn it to wider uses, does not cross most politicians' minds. Still hypnotized by dreams of a dynamic world or of absolute authority, they deal in force and power, not in persuasion and happiness. This criticism does not apply only to reactionary politicians, but to progressive ones also, and even to those who frequently state their belief in evolution as against revolution. They mean by this only that they will proceed by democratic constitutional changes, taking human nature as they find it. They do not mean, indeed, they fiercely resent, a close and scientific attention to the sources of life, character, intelligence and emotion. In so far as our politicians lay claim to being scientific at all, they put forward the theory of economic determinism. This, again, though in some ways a step forward, is limited by the eighteenth century psychology which is its foundation.

Evolution has produced its own philosophies. There is first that pessimistic determinism to which I have alluded, which sees in the wars of the species the inevitable driving force of all personal and social behaviour. This is a perfect argument for Liberal laziness, as Christian spiritual authority is for Conservative oppression. In reality it is merely nature worship. Whatever civilization men erect, according to this view, the inevitable laws of struggle and survival of the fittest will break through artificial barriers. Nature may be red in tooth and claw, but she is all-powerful.

On the other hand, we find the hopeful but mystical theories of the vitalists, such as Bergson. From them in large measure we derive that belief in creation which is very prevalent in our time. Impressed by the marvellous development of organic (living) matter, and puzzled by its differences from mechanism or what is called dead matter, the vitalists proposed a belief in the life force, a creative genius breathing through man and the animal world, driving them to imagine more beautiful and interesting forms of themselves, and so, by persistent efforts, to create them. In Bergson this philosophy leads to emphasis on instinct or intuition as the instrument of Divine creative evolution, and to scorn of the rational activities of human beings as an obstruction to these Divine purposes. Life is all-compelling, glorious, intoxicating, driving us on till we become oblivious of doubt, pain, or danger. In Bergson's own phrase it has the magnificent quality of a cavalry charge. It is scarcely to be wondered at, therefore, that the creative purpose as it spoke through the mouths of its chief and secondary apostles, was in favour of slaughtering Germans and against those who struggled, in a difficult time, for the peace and brotherhood of men. In practice the Bergsonian philosophy differs very little from Nature red in tooth and claw, for its call to man to abdicate from the reasoning faculties leaves man not the servant of Divine creation speaking through intuition, but rather the prey to passions that drive him hither and thither or can be exploited by the holders of power at will.

Bernard Shaw's version of creative evolution tries to surmount this difficulty. For him a life lived for creation is a life of happiness, but as he expresses his philosophy in *Methusaleh*, it is the intelligence rather than the instinct of man which is the creative principle. In *Methusaleh* the Ancients grow arms and legs and move matter at will by the direct power of thought. Sex, and its emotional sublimation in the arts, is merely a few years' delight to adult children. Parental love is unknown, for people come adult from eggs. Similarly, the bodily processes of digestion have been refined and in the end discarded in favour of some nobler mechanism. All of this has the asceticism, not merely of the rationalist but of medieval and oriental religions.

Clearly Shaw hates nature, and thinks her a bungler, which is odd in a supporter of creative evolution. But his finicking daintiness is not more helpful than the fictitious robustness of Bergson. Why say with Shaw that the body is all wicked because it sometimes goes savage and fights ? Why say with Bergson that the intellect is wicked because it may be wrongly used as a barrier to creative instinct ? Digestion is not disgusting, nor is sex silly, and we cannot afford to discard parental emotion. Neither can we in social or individual life do without the faculty by which we weigh good against evil, plan for the future, invent and devise mechanisms and systems external to our own bodies.

To resolve this perpetual dualism is an essential step, if we are to make progress and civilization in the place of an ever-swinging pendulum between rigidity and chaos. There is no antagonism between reason and instinct, and creative evolution proceeds by both. Reason itself is an instinct, taking its origin from animal curiosity. There is as close a connection between the sniffing of cats, the prying fingers of monkeys, and the highest flights of scientific discovery, as there is between animal sex and the rare beauty of love poetry. Out of parenthood came the patriarchal system, then a larger community life and the vast mechanisms of nations. All our life is a superstructure built upon our animal passions. It does not follow that either the superstructures or the passions are worthy of scorn or suppression.

On the contrary, our life proceeds by the interplay and interlocking of instinct with the huge structures it creates. When these structures turn upon instinct with mockery and suppression they decay. When instinct turns aside in despairing anarchy from their rigidity, it destroys where once it brought the flowing sap of life.

Modern physics, chemistry, and psychology have, I believe, a very great contribution to make to the philosophy and politics of human happiness. To be dominated by biology would be as foolish as to cherish superstitions of mechanism and economics. We learn from biology that breeding and environment are of very great importance in determining capacity and happiness. Modern physics and chemistry and psychology have gone a step further in breaking down the barriers between man and his universe. The difference between living and dead matter is dissolving. The chemistry of animal bodies is seen to be not more mysterious and remarkable than that of the water, the air, mineral compounds or green grass.[1] There is nothing in the world that is lumpish and dead in the eighteenth century sense, or in the sense of the vitalists. The world is not matter set moving or made alive by a spiritual force like gravitation or the soul. Thus there are not forms of matter that are more material and other forms more spiritual. Matter itself is energy, composed of whirling atoms. Energy whether in a ray of light or

[1] Cf. the remarkable results in high energy chemistry. Reports of the British Association. Work of Professor Baly *Times*, 7th September, 1925. "It is curious to notice that just now, when there is an increasing tendency among those who discuss the ' philosophic ' side of science to insist on the need of conceptions like vitalism, day by day exact workers in physiology and bio-chemistry are explaining more and more of vital phenomena on materialistic lines."

stored in food is the same thing. It is possible to get from cod liver oil in a dark winter what in summer the sunshine provides. Then again, things material are not always pushing and striving against one another, or being hurled about. They take the easiest path through space time, moving—to give only an approximate simile—like fishes in the swelling sea, or like wireless waves through the air. If we are to give, as men did in the past and will always do, an imaginative reading to physical discoveries, we should say that peace, persuasion, gentle slowness have taken the place of the physics of violence, dynamics, and fierce and restless activity. Everything, not only some things in the world, are ethereal, and everything is material. It is simply silly to talk of the mind apart from the body or the body apart from the mind.

Modern psychology in psycho-analysis, hypnotism, suggestion, the study of animals, of young children, of lunatics and criminals, has been inquiring more and more deeply into what we call the mind and the imagination, and their relation to the body and the external world. Bodily habits, early impressions and suggestions are seen to be the foundations of mind and character, organic matter is found to remember and retain impressions, more especially sudden fears, when they have long passed away from rational consciousness. Twisted instincts predispose to malevolence, to crime, to fancies and delusions of varying intensity. Very early education of the emotions seems vital to balanced and happy activity. All this psychology has been more and more applied of late to crime and punishment; to the cure of fear paralyses; to the nurture and education of children. It is rather a salutary corrective to the stress laid by biology on pure heredity or economic and geographical environment. Mental and emotional environment are seen to have enormous influence on highly developed structures like human beings. Moreover, it is by elaborate nurture and education that the more complex human beings are enabled to survive, be useful and perpetuate themselves. They are not necessarily weaklings, even in body, any more than the smallest seedlings that so often produce the finest flowers, and it is well that we should intervene like the gardener to mitigate the struggle for existence. To intervene by forbidding or commanding parenthood is a more doubtful proposition. It is, in many cases, advisable. But psychological and physical nurture can and should be given to all. In these and in other ways we lay a conscious hand on the blind process of natural evolution, and nothing that is honoured by being called inevitable, age-long, natural, should deter us. These are merely relative terms, we are the judges pro and con of any argument and mere worship of a shibboleth should not hold us back.

To sum up, the quest for human happiness becomes more difficult as we realize that man cannot be treated either as the chosen of God or a rational being. Everything is relevant to his life, and so to happiness, from his food and surroundings to his dreams and knowledge about the world. We can, however, make a rough picture from our present knowledge of the balance of instincts and activities which make an average well-developed human being. We can, by economic, political, and educational institutions seek to build such human beings, being careful to leave room for variety or oddity. The materials and opinion for such an effort of social creation lie scattered among scientific experts, who would be willing to help, but are too close to their specialization for synthesis.

Our rulers and candidates for rulership on whom should fall the duty of framing a policy and philosophy in our bewildered age are stupid, heartless, and muddled beyond belief. This need not be emphasized in the case of the holders of power whom we see slaying, burning, pillaging, playing recklessly with all that is cruel and destructive in man or the physical universe. But what of those others who wish to be our leaders, many so warped that they know no generous passions, some so ignorant that they will not believe they do not know, others caught by exploded dogmas, and so muddle-minded that they think they can hold at once several that are mutually exclusive. These are they who claim to be in the vanguard of progress. Politicians for instance, who at one and the same time hold in Roman Catholicism the most virulent form of spiritual tyranny, and in Marxism, the most virulent form of economic determinism, spreading over all a diffused and roseate glow of Rousseauistic sentiment. Men whose declared religion holds that physical force is a crime and that physical suffering does not matter speak of revolution and the class war to give bread and material comforts to the masses, and see no contradiction in their language. Again, upholding a belief in the nobility of the workers and the wickedness of the other classes, they seek to alter those economic conditions which, by their second dogma, have given to the workers that virtue of which they boast. If economics determine character, and to be rich is to be wicked, then surely, though I speak but with a woman's logic, the poor will grow wicked if they become rich. The generosity that is said to spring of poverty, the virility derived from close contact with " nature " and the struggle of life will surely disappear. Would it not be better if, instead of giving forth starchy dogma and windy orations, somebody were to do a little close thinking about the rock-bottom needs and possibilities of human nature? Out of this might come a philosophy—or a religion if we must have the word—appropriate to resolve the dangers and anxieties of our time.

# III

The foregoing chapters have perhaps convinced the reader that there have existed in the world a great many theories of conduct and a great deal of confusion as to the ultimate ends of life. It will not be an easy task to make all these people happy. Some of them, of course, want to be unhappy, and therefore we shall be doing our neighbourly duty by them if by word and action we help them to that end. I do not suggest active persecution of such people, the shocking spectacle of the happiness of others will suffice.

There seem, also, to be a dozen definitions of this human being whose happiness we so ardently desire. Are we to aim at the happiness of the Cave Man, or the Greek or the Christian, the gentleman, the plutocrat, or the son of toil? Whose definition and morality shall we adopt?

Since I believe in the value of scientific knowledge, I will try to take a simple definition applicable to all, though, of course, they will all refuse to accept it. A human being is a certain kind of conglomeration of processes and chemical reactions which in relation to stimuli and environment produce certain instincts and desires. Of these desires the most peremptory are the need of food and drink, next the needs of activity, sex and parenthood. The last two are distinct and not to be confounded in one impulse. Specifically human is the power of acquiring very complex habits and that form of the instinct of curiosity which, when it acquires knowledge, stores it and hands it on from father to son. Therefore, in the human being we are dealing with a creature whose purely animal reactions are conditioned by a considerable amount of knowledge and technique that have been either almost imperceptibly acquired from the parents or the communal stock of learning, or deliberately learnt by the particular human being himself. This definition of the human being will be decried by the orthodox Christian or moralist as one which takes a low view of humanity, since it derives all from the material and has not due regard for the corruption of sin and the necessary striving upward towards pure spirituality. But as we have already seen, in the light of modern physics and psychology, the mind and matter division is obsolete and nonsensical. The so-called lower impulses are not sin, nor need this agonized battle between human nature and the pagan animal world continue on its old religious and mystical basis. The preying of the animal species one upon another is not wicked, but conditioned by the necessities of their lives. Among all species human beings have displayed the greatest adaptability, variety, and ingenuity and may legitimately claim to be in command of the world. Their instincts for murder and destruction are relics of past struggles—no more. What we have to make plain to modern people is that the advances of knowledge and the possibility of security enjoin on us an ethic of positive creation rather than the old-fashioned, negative struggle for existence with its correlatives in fear moralities and religions. This ethic demands nothing less than the unity of the human race. In laying down the basis of the State, therefore, we must not be bound by old moralities, but attempt a more scientific and impartial attitude which will leave new moralities free to develop and display their worth. We are dealing with a chaotic world in which notions picked up at random have produced an infinite variety of human types, people of muddled thoughts, confused and thwarted impulses, badly bred, badly handled, badly taught from early youth. This is a source of great inconvenience to the legislator who must—does, in fact—often wish that he could once more arbitrarily impose the Christian synthesis.

Other modern legislators, such as the Bolsheviks, try to impose a new synthesis regardless of the traditions and habits of the majority of the human beings that they govern. Even their revolutionary theory of civilization, we may note, is out of date by a couple of hundred years. Apart from the propagandist bias of its schools, it teaches a dogmatic materialistic determinism that derives from the eighteenth century, has not grasped the significance of evolution and biology, nor of modern theories of matter and psychology.

The same may be said of America which is a pure eighteenth century State, whose God is the First Cause and whose religion is based on the argument from design as advanced by eighteenth century preachers. These divines were always concerned to show how the natural laws discovered by science displayed and glorified the wisdom and ingenuity of the Creator. The prosecution of Evolution in America is perfectly logical, for the bulk of its people have never grasped it. Their view of science goes no further than medicine, motorcars, and mechanical warfare. That science can say anything about human character is to them a new and horrible notion. The voice of hundred per cent America spoke through the lady who said to Freud : " In Austria you may dream those selfish dreams, but in America even in our dreams we are unselfish."

We must remember, then, in all considerations of individual rights that we are dealing with very great differences in environment and acquired habit, and therefore very different impulses and desires. A community of people who have lived a hundred years with industrialism differs greatly from a race of peasants who for the first time set eyes upon a motor-car. So every human being is compounded of parentage, traditions, environment, and education. It follows that the deliberate creation of certain types of human beings is not an impossible task and one which I shall consider later. At present it is sufficient to say that such a task cannot be undertaken in a revolutionary and iconoclastic spirit. We must beware of State imposition of religious syntheses, even new ones, and concern ourselves with defining the elementary rights of every type of human being. Evolutionary processes are slow, and there never will be an age in which all the citizens are so enlightened as to bear no marks of the superstitions of past times. It is vital, therefore to conceive of a State which legislates impartially for all, is not to be seized by a few of one type as a mechanism of oppression, and will never persecute minorities or individuals unless there is overwhelming evidence for that course. This last proviso is necessary, for we cannot permit those whose ethics enjoin wholesale murder to indulge their impulses—and this should apply to nations and classes as well as to individuals. Nor can we permit in a community where all have an ample share of what is necessary for life that men and women should rob one another of private possessions. Our laws must involve a certain check on the outworn instincts of greed and fear, and their derivatives hatred and destruction. They can only do this if they and our economic and social system provide the security and liberty which alone render those impulses useless. It is obvious that education will be needed to supplement legislation, for it is not possible in one moment to make life secure for everybody. But from security in small groups we can pass on to larger groups and so ultimately to all human society, provided each group in its turn will do its part towards the eradication of fears. At present within our own society people holding one set of beliefs dread and try to oppress people who hold others. Thus the employer tries to starve men whose opinions he fears ; Roman Catholics would like to imprison birth-controllers ; Christians try to suppress free thought or free love ; militarists torture pacifists : and quite recently men tortured women who aspired to political freedom. This all happens because we have not the right conception of State activity and of the rights of individuals. We live under worn-out laws and customs belonging to the Christian synthesis and manipulated by the possessors of wealth.

The first and most elementary principle of a society that wants to make people happy is to satisfy the primary instincts of human beings. It sounds very simple, but our own society completely fails to accomplish this simple object. The first need by our definition was food : millions of our people do not get enough to eat. " Life, liberty and the pursuit of happiness " were to be individual rights under the American Constitution, yet in America also people are starving. And the right to life, or food, is not merely a quantitative question.[1] We have not merely to give enough of just any kind of food, but the food must be pure, well adjusted to our needs, nourishing and well prepared. What would be said of a chemist who maintained that he could make a chemical compound with just any quantity of

[1] I take food as symbolical of all primary bodily needs, e.g. reasonable warmth. housing, clothes, medical care.

the particular substances he was to combine? What if, not content with that, he were to add that the spirit or soul of hydrochloric acid or whatever it was, was so magnificent that it could rise superior to defects in its chemical composition? Yet this is the sort of nonsense we talk when we are dealing with human mechanism. Fortunately, hydrochloric acid is class-conscious, and takes exactly what it needs to sustain its composition. Nor does it take more. Quantitatively food is important because men, women, and children are starving. Qualitatively food is important, first, because the eating of wholesome well-prepared food is one of the rights and joys of civilized human beings, and second, because by right feeding we can maintain the highest of our present standards of human health and vigour and probably improve upon it, thus adding to the delight of life by greater grace, suppleness and beauty of human bodies. Before the reader turns in annoyance from the childish simplicity of these sentences, will he or she reflect on the changes of government and economic organization that will be required to make them come true. The elementary right to life is explicitly denied in our society by those who make international trade competition the basis of wages. As a state, as individuals they say, we have no right to happiness, we must struggle with others for our existence. The right to life is also denied by those who pretend to affirm it when they attack the limitation of families. They demand that human beings be born though their parents may not have the wherewithal to maintain the structure of a growing human body. They do this on the ground advanced by our hypothetical chemist, that the soul rises superior to material circumstance. Besides the souls of dead babies, if duly baptised by the right brand of magic, will go to a better world. If they die before the magic is applied, or the magic is wrong, they will roast for ever to please a beneficent Deity.

Even supposing society admits the right to life, for there are signs that the public conscience is awakening, we have then the vast problem of reorganizing our food supply. We must procure enough milk or other wholesome food for all the young children and good food for all adults, not only a privileged few. We must regulate producing, buying, importing, packing, and preserving. The farmers, the meat trusts, the millers, the bakers, the cooks and restaurant proprietors must be taught to listen to food specialists, doctors, and mothers. Mothers themselves will need teaching : and cooking, not necessarily done by mothers, will become an important art and science. Think of the problem of persuading the typical old-fashioned feminine woman that both in the home and restaurants she runs— (for there are now many such enterprises run by women) scientific attention to balanced meals must replace snacks, stewed up and over-cooked rubbish, tinned foods, and cheap dried preparations. At present, even well-to-do women are far too much inclined to accept as food all that they buy at the grocers and to give it regardless of consequences to themselves and their family.

Health reports from New York on children in their teens who did not come from poverty-stricken families showed that an alarming proportion of these young people suffered from defects which began with digestive troubles due to wrong feeding in childhood. Other defects also could have been remedied but were left to become chronic and difficult of cure. The parents were either ignorant, or careless, or the food supply was being run in the interests of profit and not in the interests of human life. A dull and utilitarian idea of the basis of society ? Perhaps, but I doubt if anyone who has tended young children will say so. In this matter of food, those who conduct the State are *in loco parentis* to the citizens, and it is their bounden duty to see that not one of them lacks what is necessary to his health and growth. Nobody should vote for any politician who has not a well-considered scientific policy on a pure and plentiful food supply, its relation to trade and the numbers of the population. Put the present Parliament an examination test. I wonder how many would get through ? Minds that soar in the regions of bomb-dropping, the " glories of our blood and state ", our brethren in the far-flung British Empire, must not be tethered down to boric acid in the butter or boron in the bread.[1] The cynic will

[1] Recently the Imperial butter importers protested against the unfair advantage given to Danish butter by purity regulations, and in *The Times*, 28th July, 1925, the Bakers frankly tell the Government that they mean to go on

say that we needs must conquer to maintain
our food supply. Such cynicism is merely a
cloak for incompetence. To take by armed
conquest is spasmodic and temporary, the
conquest of public opinion alone is enduring.
A sound food policy spells peace, birth-
control, an eye to the developing needs of other
peoples besides ourselves, international control
of food-growing and raw materials. Bring
in the whole world, not a group or a federation,
especially not only the British Empire. On
no other basis can the primary right of the
human body to food be secure even in the most
powerful of modern communities. I do not
believe that I speak here the language of

poisoning the public with boron, because the public is ignorant.
They say further that they supported the Conservative
Government because they expected it to mind its own
business, e.g. deal with armaments and not the food supply.
Cf. also the recent outcry about arsenic, which had been
put into apples, without knowledge or consent of the unfortunate consumers, and the controversy regarding jam,
etc., in *The Times*, 20th–22nd September, 1926. Sir Kingsley
Wood, speaking for the English Conservative Government,
maintains that the housewife should not be encouraged to
rely upon State regulation in these respects. Such a position
implies that we shall go back to home preserving, hand-
mill grinding, and home baking, to which, in fact, many
women have already been driven.

Utopia, for everywhere in individuals and classes all over the world, the belief in the right to life is stirring. Year by year, in the teeth of the short-sighted economy preachers, we add to the functions of the Health and Education Departments [1] ; and the fall of infant mortality and improvements of public health are evidence of a passionate belief patiently applied by large numbers of people to the conquest of death, suffering, and disease. The most powerful weapon in the hands of the locked-out wage-earner is the dawning belief of mankind in the right to life. We do not suffer like Christians, we mobilize our forces to the attack. The employer is but a symbol of the enemy, a cypher in the history of what we are accomplishing : we are moving forward to the conquest of all that once we feared, and deified it because we feared it. Let our thoughts and words have the courage which our actions already proclaim.

But the conventional moralist will protest,

[1] This was written before the economies of the Conservative Government in England, 1925–6. Public indignation over these economies was great, but powerless against the Conservative majority in the Commons, which is out of all proportion to the number of their supporters in the country.

what about excesses of eating and drinking
and the necessary balance to be preserved in
this respect if we are to be happy. Here again,
I think we are dealing with a problem that will
ultimately prove illusory. In the first place,
it is idle to base our whole morality on the
probability of excess, when only a small
minority of the people are in a position to
attain it. Their number would be less at
first in a more equal society. Secondly, excess
in almost every instinctive activity is the direct
result of previous prohibition or starvation.
The very intensity of our hunger (treated by
the religious as a deadly sin) is simply derived
from the difficulty of the animal in obtaining
food. Most of us find from experience that
those that over-eat are people in whom there
still lingers the fear of starvation. A generation or two of adequately fed ancestors leading
secure lives is a better safeguard against greed
than negative teaching. Those who fear most
are most prone to hate and destroy. Those
who have newly acquired wealth are most
prone to over-display. The psychological
arguments against prohibition of alcohol are
the ones most worth consideration. Nations

which have cheap alcohol and people to whom wine or beer is a customary drink, acquire in time a natural immunity to excess. I do not mean that drunkenness does not harm them, but that they are but little tempted to drunkenness. Sudden prohibition is a stimulus to instinct which, baulked of that particular form of savagery, will find another that is perhaps more harmful. Drink is not wicked in itself, merely its excesses destroy the body and bring harm to other human beings. The right course would be not to prohibit but to provide and encourage other pleasures and to assist education by making drink not too cheap or easy of access. I would pursue this course with all pleasures that are quite definitely harmful by expert, scientific standards. New and dangerous pleasures of this type—such as drug-taking to Western peoples—I would attempt to exclude, as we attempt to exclude such terrible diseases as bubonic plague. But if an individual were resolutely set on self-destruction by any of these means, we could do no more than isolate him from those to whom he might bring harm and count him lost to the community like the criminal and the insane. Let me make it quite clear that I think it part of the legitimate pleasure of men and women, especially the young, to drink and dance to intoxication from time to time. We should neither deliver them from evil nor lead them into temptation. But the education, daily life and work of all human beings should be such as to render this no more than a recreation like games and certain forms of sport. Neither drinking, dancing, nor sport would be the central pleasure of life to those who had minds and instincts fully developed and freedom for their exercise. One word as to other pleasures that may bring bodily harm. Dangers and risks voluntarily undertaken in sport or games should not be discouraged. They involve a strengthening not a sapping of will and vitality. It is a mistake to imagine that feebleness and passivity are the qualities required to preserve an ideal state. Obviously sport must not minister to cruelty, but in the developing society we are imagining those forms of sport which do so would gradually lose their interest, and die out.

The human instinct for activity has produced

all the work which has built up civilization just as the instinct of curiosity has discovered and shown how to utilize all the knowledge on which civilization is based. Both instincts have been exercised to the pleasure and delight of man in opposition to the teachings of religion. Work was laid upon Adam for a curse because he and Eve aspired to knowledge. Both of them could have remained in the bounteous idleness and ignorance of Paradise. It is sound and logical for a religious society to regard as inferiors or as rebels those who minister to its comforts by work or by knowledge. Christians living within the community I am attempting to describe would be at liberty to continue in that opinion, always provided they took their share in the curse of Adam by contributing work for communal needs.[1] We need not ask them to risk mortal sin by contributing to our stock of knowledge, for the contribution might not be worth their damnation.

It is only quite recently that people have realized that a great many men and women work, as children run and play, from a sheer

[1] Preaching Christianity is not work by this definition.

love of activity, and that they do not cease to work when their immediate individual or family needs are satisfied. Piece by piece we uncover the fundamental instinctive life of human organisms that our false standards have overlaid, as a beautiful fresco is uncovered from the whitewashings of the Puritans. I am not trying to say that all work in the doing of it is a pleasure, or that the more work we do the more we like it. Clearly, the majority of mankind are overworked, and their work is monotonous. Therefore fatigue produces the natural reaction of disgust. Yet how many people, even those engaged in hard and dull work, would avail themselves of the opportunity never to do a stroke of work again? Even those who escaped from uncongenial work would speedily get busy on something else. And how many men and women in England at the present time are suffering from a sense of degradation and despair because they are unemployed, not wanted, having no part in the communal life of labour for human needs? This, although unemployment pay and the help of relations may maintain them at a standard of life not much below that to which they have been accustomed ? True, in the normal course of things, the State exacts work from the citizen, for without work a community cannot be maintained, but this is far less of an external discipline in our society than most people imagine. Many people enjoy dull work done in fellowship with others, a great number recognize even routine or mechanical work as an essential service and therefore it gives them pleasure. To others work in itself is a pleasure and even a privilege.

Simpler than that is the labourer's love of the soil and the crops, or the mechanic's proud devotion to a machine. Remove the shadow of starvation and overwork and the grudge against an employer and these pleasures would be increased. Every healthy child will toil and construct with remarkable patience and concentration for the sheer delight of activity and the pleasure of running to his parent at last for approval of the creation of his brain and hands. This could be our attitude to the work of adults. Public opinion should encourage creative pride in all forms of activity that minister to life or to the improvement of life's quality. We should judge men and women by what they create rather than by what they possess or destroy. This is again an ethical principle which is stirring and spreading. Those who produce food, coal, machines, those who run mechanism, those who discover science, artists, designers, teachers, mothers, doctors are increasingly conscious that the joy of their work lies in the creative impulses which it exercises. Even those whose work cannot give this sense of creation, can, if it is useful, feel they have a part in communal creativeness. With short hours of labour they would find in leisure a means to express and employ their individual instinct of activity and creation. Thus the city worker delights in his garden, and the manual worker, if not too tired, would take pleasure in books or in art.

Creative activity in this sense is not, I think, widely felt and communally interpreted by more primitive peoples. It is in Western Europeans the product of settled agricultural and industrial habits of life combined with the increase of knowledge and education which have made industrialism possible.

The instincts of activity and of curiosity,

work, and knowledge have become in us closely interwoven. From the moment scientific discovery touched on the work problem, work lost some of its quality of a curse and achieved dignity. In eighteenth century England, intelligence applied itself to agriculture. Afterwards it was busy with industrialism. Probably at bottom it is the application of science to work and physical needs which has been the means of destroying the antagonism between mind and matter. As knowledge progresses, so work becomes more skilled and needs more knowledge and the activities involved in knowledge and work are seen to be inseparably allied. I think this is an important truth too little understood by educators, politicians, and religious people. Properly understood it would wipe out the distinction between the black-coated and manual worker and settle the whole vexed question about higher education not fitting human beings for manual work. Apart from the fact that an increase of knowledge brings to every human being a new stock of interests and pleasures, it also fits him better for doing the most elementary tasks with skill and patience. It will not detract from his physical strength if bodily health receives its right place in his training.

The exercise of the instinct of curiosity is an elementary right of every human being, man, woman, and child, and every individual should be given all the knowledge he or she is capable of assimilating. We must feed the imagination and the intellect as we feed the other organs of the human structure. Boredom and repression, in other words inactivity and atrophy, are the worst enemies of individual happiness. As a climbing plant expands, it seeks hooks and supports on which to use its tendrils. If it cannot find these, the tendrils wave helplessly and the plant flaps about in an inclement wind, a miserable and thwarted being. By the old theories of Christian education, that plant should be humble and not wish to see the world, but rather creep the earth and endure buffeting meekly. Fortunately our ideals of education are fast changing, but we are still less civilized in education than in gardening. Careless about food, the State has been a parent where teaching is concerned, and a parent of the old-fashioned type. There is in our people a great mass of superstitious ignorance, and of carefully taught humility, fear, and repressive virtue. These stand in the way of their own happiness, and the happiness of others. We all know the typical virtuous and self-sacrificing human being who can enjoy no sensible pleasure because he feels it somehow not right ; who will sacrifice and work for others, neglecting his own mental and bodily joys till he is no more than an empty shell ; then will look at you with an air of gentle pity and long-suffering if you offer him a pleasure. There are more women like this than men because they are more repressed. Inwardly, such virtuous people seethe with envy of those who enjoy what they are incapable of grasping, and with a grudge against those for whom they sacrifice that no amount of gratitude and affection can dispel.

Love for our fellow-men would not have this quality of agonized repression if we ceased to feel that to be virtuous in giving to others we must take away from ourselves. That is not true. Self-sacrifice in danger and devotion in daily work may be glorious, but only when they are inspired by the feeling that we give to create life and joy, not as a sacrifice to a death's-head skeleton of empty virtue. It is a curious paradox that a man whose life is filled with joy will lay it down more cheerfully than one who has led a thwarted and dreary existence. Similarly those who are blessed with every form of happiness, by which I mean not wealth, but sufficient food, exercise for the mind and body, the love of friends, sex love and children, are those most genuinely anxious to give happiness to others. Saints and visionaries also want others to have the happiness they claim to possess. What we have to do is not to impose our standards upon anybody, but simply to follow our own ideal of happiness for ourselves, seeing to it that we so organize the State that everybody may have the food, work, knowledge and love that are capable of making him happy if he so chooses.

At present there is a vast amount of knowledge which, if taught, would make people happier, more science, more literature, more art ; knowledge of bodily processes and sex, and of mental processes in adults and children, better history, more intelligent geography.

I gave the above examples of conduct because I wanted to make clear that the teaching

we give to our citizens is to be of the widest
and not coloured by the bias of a particular
group, as at present is the case. The Church
controls the majority of our schools, especially
in rural areas. It would like to re-establish
control over all. The Roman Catholics claim
the right to censor the advice and teaching
given in public welfare centres on the ground
that they contribute to the taxes that support
them. On this ground, the free-thinking tax-
payer might claim to censor the teaching of
the Roman Catholic State-aided school. He
does so only to demand efficiency in teachers
and sanitation in school buildings, but not to
dictate doctrine.

On similar grounds to the Catholic plea,
the pacifist might dismantle the warships of
the State-run Admiralty. We cannot wait for
common agreement as to what should be
taught, therefore there must be freedom to
teach everything and no one must persecute
others. Roman Catholics, the Anglo-Catholics,
the Mormons, the Buddhists, the Confucians,
the Communists, should all be free to teach
and parents be free to expose their children
to their influence or withdraw them from it.

Similarly, free-thinkers and scientists have a right to claim that their children should spend on evolution, psychology, physiology, literature, art, and economics, the energy which they save by not learning religious superstitions. They have a right also to demand a quite different ethical teaching. To this I will return when I speak of the rights of children. But obviously the right to be happy demands that people should in so far as is humanly possible learn what they wish to know, and exercise the talents and faculties which bring them the most pleasure.

We come next to the instinct of sex and the instinct of parenthood, which are distinct, but confused in conventional teaching and thought. These are so important as to require a separate chapter. Here let it suffice to say that there are no instincts less harmful or more productive of delight in the whole range of human instincts and emotions than the desire for sex-love and the desire for children. Neither are completely denied to men in our community, nor to all women, but they are made into burdens instead of supreme joys.

Let us leave then the human being in

general with his right to the joys of life, activity, and knowledge, and turn to consider the happiness and co-operation of human beings in their sexual and parental functions.

# IV

## THE RIGHTS OF HUMAN BEINGS

### SEX AND PARENTHOOD

There is no instinct that has been so maligned, suppressed, abused, and distorted by religious teaching as the instinct of sex. Yet sex-love is the most intense instinctive pleasure known to men and women, and starvation or thwarting of this instinct causes more acute unhappiness than poverty, disease, or ignorance. I said that no men, with the exception, of course, of priests and other people of curious ethical standards, deprived themselves completely, or were deprived by the community, of their use of sexual functions. But traditional morality and early teaching, combined with the subjection of women, have robbed men of the spontaneous delight and vigour which should come to them through sex-love. A man is taught never to indulge it—the very word indulge is repulsive

—until he has found a woman with whom he is prepared to spend the whole of his life, and has been to Church for a special ceremony allowing him to possess her and forcing her to obey him. Receiving what is virtually a slave, he is then told to approach her only in the spirit of holy reverence. Never again must he look affectionately upon or approach another woman. Till recently no serious restrictions were laid upon men in regard to their lawful wives, but the improved position of women has led many religious people, including some Anglo-Catholics, to propose quite a new ruling, namely long periods of chastity within marriage, if it should be necessary for health, or other reasons, to limit the number of the family. The Roman Catholics openly advocate widespread celibacy for men and women, which is, for them, the most holy life and the only legitimate escape from parental responsibility. This teaching therefore quite clearly denies that sex is either a necessity or a lawful pleasure to men or to women and allows its indulgence only when the perpetuation of the race is desired. This is a perfectly natural result of the worship of fertility associated with agricultural superstitions. Yet anyone capable of examining his or her instincts without regard to prejudice associated with past environments finds that there is a clear division between the impulse to sexual enjoyment and the desire to have children. The primary motive involved in relations between men and women is the simple impulse towards sexual pleasure. This in primitive and ignorant communities obviously had a natural result in the responsibility of parenthood. Parental delights were not foreseen, but followed on experience. Experience in turn established a conscious tradition that the lack of offspring was a curse and a sorrow, their presence a blessing and a delight. Thus the conscious desire for parenthood arose as something separate from the sexual impulse. That there is any unconscious drive towards parenthood— any paternal or maternal instinct—is disputed. I think that there is, but that it is related rather to the phenomena of organic growth than to sex. But this is a subject for later discussion.

Because parenthood involved responsibility and pain, it was seized upon by ascetic religion as the sole justification of sexual intercourse. The major errors of Christian teachers seem to me always to arise from the insistence on ends while suppressing and thwarting the natural and pleasant means to those ends. They are so intent on proving that human life is miserable, that they cause every result desired to be reached through pain. If it be possible to arrive by pleasure that route must be barred. This principle has been applied throughout government and education in Christian countries. Therefore our society has insisted on the duties of fathers and mothers, which were to many people the less pleasant part of the instinctive relations of men and women, and at the same time made every effort to poison and destroy the impulse to sexual pleasure. Expressions of parental feeling in a distorted form pervade our social customs and institutions, but it is important to notice that the impulse to sexual pleasure has never yet had its rightful place in shaping our society, because it has not been allowed recognition. The loss we have suffered is beyond measure, but happily not beyond repair. Sex is not only the source of some of the finest poetry and art, of heroisms, sacrifices, dreams ; it is also the source of a very important human experience. In sex-love, through physical sympathy and intimate union, we draw into ourselves as in no other way the understanding of another human personality, and the knowledge that two very different creatures can live together in exquisite harmony. Such an experience alone, widespread, would be worth ten million platforms blaring pacifism. It gives, as nothing else can, the beauty of human partnership in love, of mutual abandonment of distrust for mutual joy. Christianity, it is true, enjoins that the " twain become one flesh " ; it has need to enjoin and enforce this, since all the rest of its teaching goes to prevent so miraculous a consummation. Yet supreme unions exist : they exist in spite, not because, of orthodox Christian doctrine.

More important for us all than even a fuller exercise of sex-functions is to realize that these functions are neither wicked nor obscene. Every one of us, man or woman, has been warped and corrupted in our innermost being by such teaching. Even those who repudiate the Christian synthesis and imagine themselves free of all prejudice, are a mass of tormenting inhibitions, doubts, and inconsistencies when they approach sex. Their

imaginations remain filled with false notions
of restraint and refinement ; they break
free and alternate between coarseness and self-
pitying disgust. Moralists persist in imagining
that those who speak of sex above a whisper
are concerned only to advocate free love and
excess. It is something quite different, it is
the abandonment of a pernicious mental
attitude, that we are demanding. No amount
of licence can cure our *malaise* in sexual
matters so long as those who break loose
continue to pay even lip-service to the notions
of naughtiness, bawdiness, and sin. For
these are only the reverse of abstention and
asceticism, and nobody can feel them who is
not at heart a puritan still.[1] After the manner
of repressed instincts set free sex is now stalking
society seeking whom he may devour, and
devouring many. You will not stay his ravages,
any more than the ravages of hatred and fear,

---

[1] The French are commonly supposed to be free and
civilized in sex matters. On the contrary, though their
conduct may be free, the game is played according to rigid
old-fashioned conventions, lover, wife, and husband feeling
stereotyped emotions. Pleasure is deliberately enhanced
by insistence on spiciness and sin. The purity of young
girls and the chastity of their mothers are sacrosanct to
Frenchmen, who are too conventional to understand freedom.

by chaining him up and giving him a good beating. Indeed, if you approach him without prejudice and menace you may find him neither so destructive in his antics nor so hideous in his physiognomy as you imagined. He is far less dangerous to the human structure than drunkenness. Mystic horror has led us to exaggerate the potency of sex and therefore to suppose that to leave a man and woman together in isolation is to ensure what our law so confidently and comically terms " misconduct ". Yet in the early days of free developing youth that is the least likely thing to happen. And a right education of young people, together with the claims which work and the exercise of their other functions will make upon their energies, would ensure the postponement of full sex-experience until an age at which it will not injure their development. By a right education I do not mean repression, but the imparting of many kinds of knowledge and the direction of all impulses to a happy life of varied activity. When men and women first embark upon sexual experience, I make no doubt that they will be occupied with it constantly and experiment freely. That stage

134

does not last, for the selectiveness based upon experience very speedily sets in. In this, greater freedom for women will play an important part. For, just as the moralist thinks everybody is out for free love, so does he think that free love means that no man or woman will ever refuse sexual favours to a person of the opposite sex. Yet large numbers of men and women who have freedom to experiment are not only most selective in love, but ultimately marry and never look at another man or woman for the rest of their lives, especially if they do not feel themselves compelled to this course of conduct. Others seek occasional adventures outside a permanent partnership. Others again do find that any permanency is distasteful. I incline to think that these people would prove to be rarer than either the prudish or the prurient imagine. After all, there are other pleasures besides sex, though one might scarcely think so when one hears the Puritans and the Freudians talking.

What is there in this suggested freedom that is so dangerous and wicked other than its opposition to our traditional prejudices? It would strengthen and broaden rather than

weaken and damage character ; it would add
to our lives great variety and happiness.
It would make the friendship of men and
women a real thing rather than a strained
relation for ever hovering on the brink of an
abyss towards which neither dare cast his eyes.

We have been taught that incurable disease
is the penalty of freedom, even that it is the
Divine punishment of mortal sin. This is
another of those superstitions, now exploded,
which ignorance has set up as a barrier to joy.
Do we forbid our children to have playmates,
because from one or other of them they may
catch scarlet fever ? Sexual diseases, however
repulsive, are like any others, and are open to
cure. Already science has mastered them, and
but for our superstitious morals, we should by
now have eradicated them completely.
Obviously, where disease is present, our ethical
code should enjoin honest avowal and temporary
abstention. One may point out that neither
the Law nor the Church of our Christian
State enjoins this even in marital relations.
On the contrary, our social ethics prescribe
a conspiracy of silence that protects husbands
and treats the bodies of wives and possible

children as chattels of no account. It ought to be an offence involving the indignation of the whole community and possibly the penalty of the law for anyone to infect another, man or woman. Private notification which would be followed by private free treatment should certainly be compulsory. If this were so, it might be safe and just to make it a punishable offence to infect another human being. But all legal action in these matters is likely to lead to tyranny and abuse, and our best safeguard lies in an enlightened public opinion. It should, I think, continue to be an offence to force actual sex experience on the very young, but an offence usually calling for pathological treatment rather than castigation. I would not legislate against literature and pictures ; the minds of freely taught people are quite adequately safeguarded. Repressive laws invariably lead to the prosecution of works of art and to the free circulation of cunning suggestiveness.

A discussion of sex involves us immediately in a discussion of the rights of women, for it is the rise of women to a position nearing equality which has caused the most perplexing of our social problems. When one of the sexes acquires a dominant position it seems invariably to attempt to compel the other to lead a life conditioned entirely by the functions of sex and parenthood. Thus it is said that in ancient Egypt women were dominant, that they conducted all the business of life whilst the men tended house and children, even bringing up the babies on milk from birth.[1] In such a society men curried favour by means of sex and self-adornment, just as women have always been obliged to do for a very long period in European history.

Teuton women according to Tacitus had a position of dominance, and in Sparta, it seems that they were, if not dominant, at least powerful. But on the whole, Greek and Roman women like the women of the Mohammedans, the Chinese, and the Christians were subject to the men. In Greece, as in traditional China, woman is not so utterly the slave of male sexual pleasure as in the Mohammedan Empire. She is respected and honoured in her functions as a mother and mistress of a household. But one may observe

[1] Vaerting, *The Dominant Sex*.

to-day among traditional Chinese that rigid separation of the life of men and women which must have existed in ancient Greece. The women have their own apartments, and though they go freely in the streets, they receive and visit no men but near blood relations. Those men who are rich enough to have leisure spend all day away from home in the company of male friends and regard their wives—whom they receive in early youth as the result of a bargain between the parents—solely as the instruments of sex and maternity. But since sex, as in Greece, is honoured rather than despised, the wife does not feel humiliated and unhappy. Her life is that of an instinctive animal, and so regarded it is not unpleasant. The life of the medieval Christian woman on the contrary was a constant humiliation. She was taught that her province was an instinctive life, and at the same time the doctrine of sin commanded her to hold her instincts in horror. Her sex relations with her husband were only sanctioned through grace and sacrament, her body after performing its maternal functions was unclean and required the blessing of the Church to restore its purity. She lived therefore in conflict and was bound to feel that if she was happy in her marital and maternal life [1] she must be committing a sin. She was more unfortunate than the Greek or Chinese woman, for she might not enjoy life as an instinctive animal, yet her only escape from a life bounded solely by sex and maternity was the self-immolation of the cloister. So torn was the blessed Angela of Foligno by this conflict between holiness and her instinctive life that she prayed God to resolve it for her. Which He did by causing her husband and children to leave this earth for the glories of Heaven.

It must have been a pleasure to the Serpent to watch his pupil Eve worm her way out of this prickly and preposterous thicket with which the medieval theologian had surrounded her. There were three clues to the conundrum, two sinful and one virtuous. The way of virtue was also the way of deceit. Woman followed all three. She cut the knot and lived by means of her sexual impulses and became a " fallen

[1] The Christian Editor of *G.K.'s Weekly*, replying to the present writer, states that the avoidance of burdens is attempting to escape life. Life and maternity in his view neither can nor should be made mainly delightful (26th December, 1925).

woman " ; she climbed out of instinct by the ladder of knowledge and became a " blue stocking " ; she invented an elaborate system of reticence, refinement, and pretence by which she got the best of both worlds and saved her soul for heaven and became a " lady ". All of these three worldly careers were open to her in the lay society which accepted Christian standards. It needed a great many apples from the tree of knowledge, however, before courage was found to step out of the Christian synthesis altogether. Yet that was the only possible action consistent with self-respect and honesty. The sooner this is realized by the women of our time the sooner will the confusion surrounding sex and married life be smoothed into harmony, and the sooner can we set about the task of building a new society and the citizens who are to compose it. To accord limited rights and freedom to women is impossible, either they must be driven right back into slavery or society accept the full consequences of their succession to the inheritance of science.

We are constantly being told that women have now got complete equality with men and being snubbed for talking feminism when the whole mental picture which most people have of woman and her functions, and which woman herself is still taught, is so false and ridiculous as to make woman's political freedom not only futile, but even, it may be, dangerous. Preserve us from a society governed by typical middle and upper class women ; it is bad enough when middle and upper class men hold the reins of power. Preserve us equally from the dominance of the timid and bigoted among working spinsters and working mothers. Preserve us, in fact, from rule by the votes of any, be it men or women, who have not the integrity and courage born of truthful teaching and honest living. The lady is the worst of the disguises of Eve, for she has corrupted the others with her example. Feminine education is said to have made great advances, but in fact it has hardly yet begun its work. Girls are taught at school and university a curriculum resembling that taught to boys, but nobody seems to realize that in this way we do no more than plaster a so-called masculine career on a character which has already been formed to femininity from early youth.[1] Insensibly,

[1] I am speaking here of early education before school age.

from the day of birth millions of mothers are still teaching their daughters feminine timidity and delicacy, a sense of inferiority, dishonesty, teaching them above all always to *seem* something rather than to *be* a real character or person.[1] Nurses, fathers, and mothers of all classes, almost without realizing it, adopt an indulgent tone to their girl babies and soften and pamper them in mind and body. Middle-class parents encourage boys to wait upon their sisters, and working people compel the girls to wait upon the boys. Both attitudes deny equality and give to both sexes a sense that the value of a girl lies in her womanhood, and not in her individuality. Think of the middle-class ladies one meets in railway trains, who exact every kind of service and respect, particularly from men, and who, as individuals, are really so worthless that they had far better not have existed. But they have learnt all the tricks and can seem important and talented on occasion, they can seem anything that will retain them a position of idleness and power.

[1] Dr. Paul Bousfield, in his *Sex and Civilization*, makes what I believe is a really profound psychological observation on this point, though I do not agree with his more Freudian explanations.

This is a sex and not a class phenomenon. Such women are virtuous in the sense that they do not exercise their sexual functions, but they would stare in amazed horror if they were told that day by day and hour by hour they live by and trade upon their sex. I am thinking of something that goes deeper than the old controversy about chivalry and economic dependence and what I say applies to a great many clever women who earn their living and believe in women's rights. Somewhere there still lurks in the mind of every woman who has not received an extremely modern education the idea that it is as women that we are important, that we are honoured and respected for that in us which is woman, and the more to be honoured and respected when—being still charming woman—like Rosalind we adopt the voice and antics or perform the work of a man. Every new profession we enter appears to us merely as another aspect or disguise in the great game of being a woman. I can hear the reactionary acclaim this as a remarkable admission. Woman will always be woman— how delightful. Yes, she will always be woman so long as that is the only thing she is taught to be. Early education of boy or girl is no more than training to act a part in life. Just as in certain respects we teach a boy manhood, so in almost all respects from early years, we preach womanhood to women. And to most of them still we teach nothing else. Here again the honesty of the Greek or Chinese attitude is superior to the Christian. The womanhood it imposes is at least genuine. Woman loves sex and loves children. She may come frankly and honestly to the marriage-bed and to child-birth. She may express her animal devotion with the outspoken language we find in Greek tragedy. The women of Troy lament that in the arms of the Greeks sex passion will prompt them to forget their fatherland, and Hecuba in her agony traces the warm impress of her dead son's body on his clothes, the marks of his prowess in the dents and hollows of his shield. Blessed abandonment to instinct in joy or in despair, binding the bodies of men and women together with innumerable tendrils of physical sympathy and understanding, opening in their souls the flood-gates of generosity, tenderness, and compassion. This is the supreme possession of the primitive woman and the vital core of her being. Therefore the Christian strikes at it with his ideal of delicate and saintly womanhood, tears from her this evil fellowship with the beasts that she may come with a broken and contrite heart to a union that is all duty and reticence.

It is curious that people who can understand the corruption of character which must result when a man is forced to earn his living by expressing opinions in which he does not believe, fail to understand this principle in the psychology of women. They are surprised at the feminine wiles and even the dishonesty and parasitism of women who have received as is thought a man's education and have an opportunity to live a man's life. They forget that though men are shockingly warped by early training the phrase " a man's life " does imply for a man a right to sexual expression. A woman's life with a man's career is built on the assumption that she does not need sex. Similarly the womanly woman who lives by sex and maternity must pretend that it is a duty and not a pleasure. One of the most serious objections raised by a whole bench of magistrates to a pamphlet recently suppressed was that it said in set terms that women should experience pleasure in marital relations.[1] A nice woman must be coy and timid and set barriers to such thoughts and feelings. A denial of motives that are thought bad and an inability to face facts are common enough results of repression in men, but they are still commoner in women. Dishonesty, then, is a necessary ingredient in Christian feminine psychology Parasitism arises also quite naturally, even in the woman who can earn her own living. She perceives first that what a masculine society values in her is the woman, not the individual worker, and second that all exercise of instinctive functions connected with sex brings with it financial support from men. Indeed, from the moment a woman in our society desires sex or maternity we compel her if we can to become dependent on a man or on men. Thus a single woman worker discovered in immorality is liable to be discharged, in which case she is often obliged to make a living as a prostitute. Similarly, women whose work may be admirable, are discharged on marriage. Put bluntly, a woman must still choose between

[1] The Sanger pamphlet : *The Aldred Case,* 1923.

instinctive slavery and instinctive starvation.
Is it astonishing that an able woman making
a career whose mind is full of the stops and
inhibitions implanted in childhood should not
reach the level of man's achievements ? It is
as if a pianist were trying to perform in gloves
or an actor to give an intimate and delicate
performance in a mask. Our whole view of
woman is still a mask between her and reality.
As she tries to tear it away the whisper of
reaction urges her not to become unsexed,
but to preserve her womanly instincts. Reaction
cares nothing for her instincts, what it really
hopes to preserve is the mask of the ignorant
pretence-prude which passes muster for a
woman. It is sex in women, not sexlessness,
that reaction fears, since the more colourless
a person the easier it is to hold her in subjection. Women *are* unsexed at present by a
steady and merciless process of elimination
that leaves them atrophied or self-denying,
advocating repression for others. Perpetual
watchfulness against the snares of sex dries
in them the springs of affection and sympathy.
Hatred of all that is associated with instinct
is so well taught that when women get freedom

they do not want to be cooks or housemaids, wives or mothers. It is not at all astonishing that they go in for Purity and Prohibition, that older feminists cannot see what sex has to do with political freedom, that all and sundry begin to feel that maternity is a nasty illness, breast-feeding a horrid bother and babies an infernal nuisance. They do but follow the blessed Angela of Foligno, who felt these things and called them holiness.

Many people will here object and say that on the contrary women are doing more year by year to tend and protect the lives of children, and that their maternal feeling is spreading through society with wholesome and beneficial results. That is perfectly true. Women are rediscovering the life of instinct in the light of scientific knowledge. But when they return to it they do so in a mood quite unlike that which tradition would teach them. I do not advocate, nor would modern women accept, a return to barbaric instinctive slavery. The human right to knowledge spoken of in the previous chapter is a right shared by women and by men, and as in the work of the community, so in sex and parenthood, knowledge plays a vital part in shaping instinctive activity. In no department of life is scientific knowledge so powerful in destroying the barriers of superstition and helping instinct to happiness and creation as in the functions of sex and parenthood. Woman's acquisition of education and her consequent rise to power make questions of sex and parenthood mutual problems that cannot be settled without the consent of both parties. That this is increasingly felt is shown by such things as the Bill for equal guardianship of children and the more or less successful move towards equal divorce laws. These laws are still stupid, but they are now nearly the same for both parties. The most striking manifestation of women's improved position is, however, the attitude of Church and State to the birth-control controversy. Nobody, not even the Roman Catholic, dares to disregard the woman's point of view on this question. Formerly it would have been said quite bluntly that the wife and mother had no rights and that the conjugal rights of the male imposed on her the bearing of any number of children. Everybody would have scoffed at imposing on a married man that degree of chastity which ensured only four children to a marriage. Yet the medieval type of Christian has been driven into that ridiculous doctrine by the freedom and independence of women, by nothing less in fact than the assertion by women of the right to be happy. The misery, degradation and disease associated with the burden of unlimited maternity combined with heavy domestic work are no more to be imposed upon women. Those who most desire to have children and care for them are also those who are most determined that this task shall no longer be an agony but a pleasure. Before we pass on to parenthood, however, let us complete the argument relating to the instinct of sex.

I do not think people realize, or will ever do so without changing their whole idea of what constitutes a woman, what sex starvation means in the ordinary lives of hundreds of thousands of men and women who earn their living.[1] The richer and more varied the

[1] In a report from Birmingham on unemployment pay (*Times*, 30th July, 1925) the following passage occurs: " A more serious aspect of the case is the apparent readiness of both men and women to undertake the responsibility of the married state on the flimsy security of the ' extended '

personality the worse the effects of repression.
Most of the trouble flows from our absolute
refusal to separate the instincts of sex and
parenthood in our social and economic structure.
Thus a young man dare not marry until he
has a good enough position to support a
wife and a family. The more skilled and
brilliant he is the less will he wish to hamper
himself by these claims and anxieties. Therefore for many years he is baulked and starved
—as all virtuous single women are—or else
he must go to a special type of woman whom
society for convenience sake forces to sell her
physical wares by direct barter. Yet men are
hungry for a fuller companionship with women
than a mere sex relation provides and they
cannot get this from casual prostitutes. Rich
men may find prostitutes as accomplished as

benefit. . . . *The peculiar frame of mind* (my italics) which
will enable a girl to leave her employment and to become the
bride of a man in receipt of 'standard' or 'extended'
benefit is difficult to understand." I see nothing either
peculiar or difficult to understand in a woman who takes
the only road society allows her to the satisfaction of her
two most vital instincts. Nor would anybody who had not
been warped by two thousand years of Christianity, and the
later superstition that economic security alone is the basis of
happiness.

the *hetaera* of ancient Greece, but poor men rarely. All use of sex outside marriage between men and young women reared to virtue means clandestine meetings and elaborate arrangements for secrecy. The penalties are still heavier for the women than the men. What can the woman worker do ? She also must look upon marriage as parenthood with responsibility and suffering. She has perhaps a bare livelihood. To marry a man of similar position means real hardship because she must not continue at work. When children are added, she sees by the example of other women that she will have to starve herself to feed them and her husband. Like the man, the more valuable she is as an individual, the less will she wish to relinquish her other activities. The incentive to continue earning and lead a secret sexual life is obvious. Yet that solution may bring misery. There is the sense of social disapproval which enforces secrecy and the perpetual dread of discovery or an accidental pregnancy. A woman may feel that in sex she is merely claiming, as indeed she is, a right and need of her nature, but guilt, disaster, difficulty lie in wait for her on every side. What hinders us from establishing a social system in which young men and women who are out in the world earning may enter into open temporary sex partnerships without harm to the work and legitimate ambitions of either? Nothing whatever except our false picture of woman and our ingrained ascetic belief that sex is wicked if enjoyed and not immediately succeeded by the pains, anxieties, and penalties of parenthood. Yet such companionship, not despised and concealed, would work great changes in the character of individuals. There would be fewer lonely, hard, and envious men and women, less anger and jealousy, more generosity and love—the one kind of love that is really worth having, loved based on understanding. The woman would not be primarily a sex creature, the man not there only to buy her favours. There would be holidays of mutual enjoyment, mutual discussion of all the problems of existence in which young and eager people delight. The day's work would be enlivened by the thought of the free and lovely companionship to come when it was over, of the other personality ready to sympathize and discuss. Such companionship arises between people of the same sex, but it is from each other that men and women draw the deepest sense of peace and self-completion. The idea of sin must be banished, as must any demand for special service or sacrifice by the woman. (Men sometimes tend to regard free love as a means to getting their socks darned cheaply.) There would be passionate griefs, disappointments and broken ideals, but none of this is so damaging to human personality as atrophy. We must have freedom and courage to learn if we are to be worth anything as human beings. And when these struggles are surmounted men and women often find they have been but the prelude to a symphony, a preparation for the most vital sex experience of their lives, which bears fruit in a union in which soul and body cry aloud : " For this, for this was I born ! "

To such a union each partner brings a knowledge of his own temperament and needs and a willingness and ability to understand the needs of the other, to such a union are added loved and wanted children. I want both freedom and honesty for men and women because I believe that neither spasmodic sex experience nor a strict marriage entered into in ignorance or frivolity can give men and women the poise and harmony which should come to them through sex. Hot-headed choice is often at fault and experience is the only trustworthy guide. Similarly impatience and egotism frequently break off a union that promises well, because the two people concerned are not able to live the open common life which might weld them into harmony. Presenting a spontaneous psychological unity to the world is a quality which distinguishes perfect sex unions. It is not always achieved at first even by people who are well matched and passionate lovers. Yet it should not involve an effort or it is unreal.

In the minds of very many people who are not conventionally moral or religious lingers the notion that since a supreme union between man and woman is possible, physical and emotional energies should be reserved until that union is found. Men frequently regret what the moralist calls pre-marital indiscretions, and pre-marital experience for women is definitely still thought a crime. In books on marriage and child-rearing by good doctors, intended for the average middle-class man and woman, one is astonished to find how traditional prejudice will prevent the authors from drawing the moral and political conclusions which flow quite obviously from their medical diagnosis.

A doctor, for instance, will follow materialistic scientific psychology, and discount original sin in the rearing of young children, but he would not apply the same principles when it comes to labour troubles, or international rivalry. An expert spinster nurse will write pages of excellent advice on the feeding of children, and sheer dogmatic idiocy when she touches upon sex teaching. Books on marriage echo and re-echo with the sensitive delicacy of woman and the necessity of avoiding shocks to her nerves.[1] I cannot but feel that something quite blunt must be said on the subject of male and female chastity and this alleged delicacy of women. Over and over again these books tell us how marriages go

[1] The books here referred to are : *Health in Children*, 1925 ; *Mothercraft*, Miss Liddiard, of the Truby King Institute at Earl's Court ; *Hygiene in Marriage*, Dr. Isabel Emslie Hutton, 1923. See also *The Child, His Nature and His Needs*. Children's Foundation, Valparaiso, 1925.

wrong through the ignorance of women and the brutality of men, and yet go on preaching the conventional doctrine of planting down two people of complete inexperience in a marriage from which neither must seek to escape. It is admitted by these moralists that physical dissatisfaction will render such a marriage miserable, and that, when the complicated physical and psychical factors are all considered, the chances of success between two utterly inexperienced persons are very remote. A happy sexual life is, in fact, in a developed personality, the product not only of strong instinct but of art and science in its use.

It is not impossible that a time may come when pre-marital experience will no longer be regarded as a crime, or even as an indiscretion. People may come to think it better for the ultimate happiness of men and women if the affections and emotions are not too deeply entangled in their first experiences of sex. The idea that we fritter away our emotions and energy does not hold good of people whose training has not led to too great concentration on the sexual aspect of their lives. On the contrary, the maladjust ments which may come at first and cause angry reactions against the person with whom they are associated, disappear as we grow more fully awake to the technique of sex, and we become more capable of an important, deep and happy sex-union. The "superstition of chastity" is a part of that same false psychology which makes moral virtue consist in emptiness and abstention. Chastity for women has been a part of ethical teaching in nearly all societies where men were dominant. It is associated primarily with property and children, and the desire to make sure of descent when it is traced through the male line.[1] This has led to the caging of women both before and after marriage under the patriarchal system. Alike in Greece, China, Mohammedan and Christian countries insistence on female chastity has prevailed. It has become dissociated from its original purpose and has been valued for its own sake, with serious and far-reaching results. In Greece we find that the goddess of chastity

[1] The legitimate uses of this desire are treated of later.

is associated in men's minds with the pursuit of hunting. Artemis herself is a huntress, pure and boyish in her athletic integrity. But she suggests also the fleet doe which she hunts, and the pleasure of man in the primitive pursuit of a woman to conquer her virginity.

Sex love thus acquires, as in Christian countries, the aspect of a chase, which ends when the woman is finally caught and subdued. The refinements of chivalrous love in medieval times express the same feeling tempered to a more exquisite sensation by ascetic delicacy. The lady is adored by her lover from afar, and to possess her would spoil the refinement of emotion. This much lauded chivalrous love is really no more than the play of vanity in man and woman and the pleasure of gloating anticipation. The same thing appears in eighteenth century intrigue. The gallant strings conquered women on to his vanity as a Red Indian strings scalps to his girdle. Love is sought, not because the woman will be a prized and honoured companion, but because it has a tang of wickedness, and a delight to vanity like that of the hunter who returns with a big bag from his day's sport. Comparisons between pursued and charming women and wounded birds or terrified wild creatures appear in the talk and writings of gallant old gentlemen of the Victorian age. The theory of woman's delicacy, her distaste for sex, her horror and dread in capture, all of them reinforced by medieval asceticism, make this pursuit peculiarly delightful and brutalizing to the male. Women have played the horrible game till they are sick of it, or so obsessed by it that they feel it to be a reality. Even those who claim to enlighten them on sex are teaching them to play it still. The psychological results are deplorable. Enormous numbers of middle-class and working women apparently still despise their husbands as people of an inferior animal nature, whose desires a woman may condone in loving-kindness but can never share. Married life is a series of shocks to delicate nerves, against which the woman erects barriers of artificial separations and refinements, continuing to play the game of coyness which she has been taught to regard as necessary to retain a man's affections.[1] For this is the lamentable consequence of the superstition of chastity, that it leads people to look on marriage as the end rather than the beginning of happiness. The hunt is over, the quarry run to earth. Woman perhaps in modern times has been the huntress. The effect is the same, excitement dies and emptiness lays a cold hand on lovers' ardours. As we have learnt not to seek happiness in this world, but to wait for it till we reach heaven, so do we dream of that perfect wife or perfect husband whom in our folly we believe the world of real men and women cannot provide. Valuing chastity above love, and the chase above its ending, we come to believe that there is no happiness which, when we hold it close and clasp it to our hungry hearts, will not turn to dust and ashes in our hands. Therefore men and women flee from deep love as from a prison and dread marriage as a snare set for their unwary feet. Therefore not only in sex love, but in every activity of life men and women

[1] Cf. the early days of marriage between Rousseau's Sophie and Emile.

develop an attitude of dissatisfaction, waiting and longing, which blinds them to the fullness and beauty which even now may be theirs.

If women really desire an individual life, freedom and a part in the cultural development of the race, they must not only fight for the right to do any man's work of which they are mentally and physically capable, they must also be more honest and frank about their instinctive nature and its functions. Why should they seek only the traditional life of a woman or the traditional life of a man ? Why try to combine these two, whose traditional philosophies are quite separate and mutually exclusive ? Because men have so long ruled the world, it does not follow that the philosophy by which they have ruled it is the correct one. Nor does it follow that if woman rules she should do so in accordance with a picture of her nature almost wholly drawn by the religion and philosophy of men. Why all this feminine delicacy ? If we are hysterical and timid about our animal desires and functions and cannot have the courage to be honest, that is a thing to be ashamed of, not a reason for boasting and special consideration. Men have pushed on to us all the reticence and virtue, we in turn push on to them all the brutality and vice. We incite them to brutality by the pretence of coldness, that we may escape the sin of the flesh by escaping the responsibility for aggression. Strength and health of body and honesty of mind would soon show that the modesty and sensitiveness of woman associated with this " shock " of marriage and her bodily changes, is as much a hysteria as the Victorian swoon at a man's declaration of love.

Clearly, in a society which assumes in woman a dislike of physical love, women can reap a great economic advantage by keeping up the pretence. They get paid for sex, because they are deemed to dislike it. Formerly the plea was just, because sex in marriage involved unlimited child-bearing, and sex outside degradation and misery, for which no amount of riches and fine clothes could compensate. Now, however, women can make men and society reward them for what is their pleasure, and on the plea of delicacy, escape even the pains of maternity. Everybody except the society butterfly and her imitators stands to gain by dropping this pretence about woman's ethereal nature and her hypocritical assumption of sole guardianship over what is civilized and moral. Women should be paid, not for sex, which, if they were honest and robust, they would admit as a pleasure, but for maternity, which, though it, too, is a pleasure, is also a responsibility and a communal service. What women from their instinctive nature can bring to civilization is a warm physical and mental companionship in place of cold and genteel condescension, and a clear and scientific statement—not moralizing and sentimental—of the claims of maternity and child life on the political and economic system.

In sex life I believe that women who were free and honest would find that they did not differ very greatly from men. They would feel strong impulses towards some men, others they would feel to be sexually tolerable, others would suggest indifference or repulsion. Women are, I believe, more selective than men, but it is less easy for them to be selective without experience. They are not, as is commonly supposed, invariably entangled emotionally and hysterically in love; like men, they have great and small passions, and can learn by experience to choose a partner for permanence and parenthood. It is said that the sex impulse in women can flourish only at the expense of maternity. I think this view derives from past times when large families completely absorbed a woman's physical strength and emotional energy, so much so that the husband frequently felt himself cheated of the love he sought in mating. This led to the painful division between maternal women and the childless women sought by men for sexual love. In actual fact a woman is as capable as a man of combining love of a mate, parenthood and physical or intellectual work. Like so many things which people insist upon treating as matters of principle, this is purely a quantitative question. It depends on the physical and mental energy of the woman concerned, the number of her children, the economic status of the family. When opponents of birth control argue that it makes of marriage legalized prostitution, they mean simply that it might enable a man and woman to continue enjoying holy wedlock because they would retain health and a freedom from too great anxiety. It is alleged by many people, who profess to speak not ethically but from science, that but for the fear of children men would be savage and brutal and exhaust their wives, and even themselves, by excess. I do not believe this is possible for healthy, hard-working people within marriage, and birth control aims above all at conserving the physical and emotional energy of the wife. Apart from this, it is psychologically true that brutality is the reaction to coldness. A real sex union does not perpetuate the emotions of the chase, and a warm and physical love from a woman in some way stills the hunger of a man for the blunt sexual experience. Some-how two people who are really one flesh have less need to be constantly proving it. If the delicate woman really desires to diminish the dreaded masculine rapacity, her artificial barriers and niceties are a gross error in psychology. The civilizing of sex, as of every-thing else, lies in the thought and emotion which give varied and supple expression to primitive passion, not in checks and suppressions of the passion itself.

The women who to-day refuse maternity and permanent marriage to earn their own living

and lead an open or surreptitious free sexual
life do so for a number of reasons. Most of
these are to be considered in dealing with the
thwarting of parenthood. Here I want to say
something about the reasons which lie in the
character of women themselves. Many of
these younger women are really irresponsible,
in the sense that they have been trained to
believe that freedom means an utter lack of
personal responsibility for anything but their
own economic existence—scarcely perhaps
even that, since parasitism is so profitable.
Parasitism they derive from the old theory of
woman's place ; and the joys of economic
freedom, which are real and important, from
the first battles of feminism. Some of them
have learnt to combine this freedom to work—
these are not meant to be hard words—with
the advantages of the lady and the prostitute.
Very few have yet understood that the real
problem of feminism is the emancipation of
mothers.[1] Knowing nothing of the science of
maternity and instinct, they think it impossible
to combine a life of intelligence, health, and

[1] Cf. the attitude of the English feminist paper, *Time and
Tide*, on what it terms the side-issue of birth control.

physical charm with the bearing and rearing
of children. In this, though they do not realize
it, they are accepting the most ancient of
religious and moral superstitions. They turn
their backs on that one thing in a woman's life
which makes it different from that of a man,
and which has been the weapon of reaction in
insisting on the protection and subjection of
women. What an appalling confession of
weakness. If we cannot have children and
remain intelligent human beings, if we must
descend into the silliness, timidity, sacrifice,
humility associated with the idiotic convention
of the mother, then, indeed, our emancipation
is a mockery. I know it is difficult. Men and
women, especially spinsters and childless
people, overlay and spoil everything for a young
pregnant woman or mother by their prating
and twaddling and false sentiment. To an
intelligent mother their talk is as stupid as the
chirruping of a society lady visiting a coal mine
is to the man who digs the coal. Unfortunately
woman after woman allows herself to be hoaxed
into thinking intelligence should be left on
the door-mat of marriage. It is such a pity that
so few intelligent women can bring themselves

to investigate motherhood and spend time and energy upon children. The class prejudices of feminists are greatly at fault. Those among them who have children have solved their problems by their economic advantages, giving their children to the care of paid working women. It is still supposed, owing to the aversion of intelligent women from the subject, that it is best for children to be with a primitive and ignorant person—a motherly body. Certainly a cold-hearted expert is harmful, but there is scarcely a moment passes in a child's life when a mistaken word, gesture, or emotion on the part of those in charge of it cannot do untold harm. Only those who know children will believe me when I say that every simple direction of a child's emotion, every answer to a matter-of-fact question, or plain physical care of the child's body, is linked to all kinds of science and the most abstruse speculations of human thought on the problems of existence, of morals, and of politics. Yet the majority of women (not necessarily of the working class) to whom the care of children is given, are so ignorant that they do not even know how to place a cot or pram so that sun and wind will not trouble the child in sleep. A real and highly trained mind, a healthy body, physical, mental, and moral courage, nerves rendered stable by the free play of instinct are essential qualities in a guardian of children, man or woman. The emotional instability of intelligent women which makes them feel that they are superior to the task of caring for children, because they are easily fatigued and worried by them, should be their shame rather than their pride. It is another phase of that supposed delicate superiority which derives from asceticism and the psychology of the chase. Unless they refuse to be bound by it any longer, their boasted freedom will disappear like scum or ripples from the surface of a pond. For we cannot all solve the problem of children by not having them.

Admittedly there are women who should be free not to have children, or free of tending them. We have to seek a philosophy suited both to the common run of people and to the exception. But to do that we must draw together all needs of women, intellectual work, sexual and economic freedom and maternity. We have to make different groups of women understand, instead of despise, one another. The first need is to raise the social, economic, and intellectual status of the mother which is at present inferior to that of the earning spinster or the independent woman who leads a free sexual life. The mother is to have time and health for intelligence and for sex enjoyment. To be capable of these last she should not be before marriage the simple, shrinking, and ignorant girl who is still too much admired and sought after.[1] Such women become the devoted tiresome mothers who do not understand their children's bodies and do infinite harm by their inhibitions and timidity to their children's intellect and morals. We need as mothers and guardians of children women who have the courage born of sexual and economic freedom and the intelligence and instinct to perceive the great possibilities of maternal work. Whatever women achieve in the arts and sciences, it is in maternity and child nurture

[1] Cf. *The Child, His Nature and Needs*, Chapter XV, and the American Press of the Middle and Far West in general.

that they can make the most important political and cultural changes. It does not follow that we should be bound by the present family life, that the mother would also be cook and household drudge. Well-to-do households even now divide this work intelligently, and by good communal housekeeping and the nursery school the division would be made by society. I see no reason why housework or cooking should be regarded even as primarily feminine occupations. Since large numbers of men have abandoned the sword and the plough, the broom and the stewpan are weapons as worthy of them as the pen and the typewriter. But I think it essential for men and women for their own benefit to have something to do with their children, because instinct evaporates if it is not developed by technical use.[1] Maternal feeling will speedily die in a woman who does nothing at all for her child but bring it into the world and maternal feeling is an important source of individual and social happiness.

[1] Chalmers Mitchell (*Childhood of Animals*) confirms this, maintaining that parental affection is not the cause but the result of parental care.

If possible every woman should do all that is necessary for her baby for a great part of the nursing period. This sounds primitive and old-fashioned, but the suggestion is based on experience. Artificial feeding is not sufficiently good yet to take the place of natural methods, but, apart from that, the handling and suckling and tending of the child are essential to a full development of maternal feeling. It is not the same thing to supervise and receive a washed and brushed-up infant to poke fun at at stated intervals. Forego pleasure and if possible other work for a few brief months, and, if you have maternity anywhere in your nature, it will come out and establish a love and understanding of the child, and so of all children, which will last till the end of your days. All this applies to those women, who, like so many men, value and develop intellect to the neglect of instinctive happiness. Quite different advice applies to the adoring, instinctive woman, who neglects husband and the outer world to make herself a nuisance to her child. She needs a developed mind, and it may be that she can best be helped by exact training in that very maternity to which her profoundest instinct leads her. The woman's problem to-day is parallel to the problem confronting all society, namely to bridge the gulf between intelligent rebels and pioneers who have climbed out of what is ordinary because its stupidity disgusts them, and those left behind, who, though sound and stable in instinct, are ignorant and intolerant in its application. If we turn now to parenthood, and apply a similar analysis, we shall find that here, too, the incredible perversion of our society has turned a spontaneous pleasure into a hardship and pain. The separation of the sex instinct from the desire for children is important not only in the interests of sexual freedom, but in the liberation of parental feeling itself. Freud seems to follow the Christians in confounding these two impulses in one, and both would probably claim that biological necessity supported them. But if we go far enough back in our evolutionary ancestry we find parenthood existing without sex—before male and female come into being. Logically, therefore, one might maintain that parenthood is not only distinct from sex but even older than sex, that it is, in fact, identical with the impulse to grow and spread through the universe, which is a striking characteristic of organic matter. The primitive root of parental feeling is thus the desire to expand the ego in space and time. That is why all substitutes for parenthood must provide substantial food for our vanity, such as world-wide or posthumous fame, great deeds, immortality of the individual soul. Bertrand Russell has said that the arguments which prove the soul immortal would also prove it to be immeasurably fat. This may well be, because, being a sublimation of the desire for parenthood, the desire for immortality simply *is* the desire to be immeasurably fat.

The intervention of sex has led to a great deal of confusion in people's minds as to the nature of parental feeling. Thus the followers of Freud, through identifying the growth principle with *libido* or sex, tend to assert that if there is a close physical affection between parent and child, this is of necessity a perversion of sexual feeling. The mother " fixes " on the son, the father on the daughter, etc. This is certainly true in abnormal psychological cases, where the parent and child concerned have inhibitions resulting from repressive education or other sexual thwarting, but it is emphatically not true as a universal proposition. Under the influence of Freudian theories, modern people are rapidly casting aside their asceticism about sexual desires, but they are developing asceticism about parenthood. They renounce any close relationship with their children because they regard this as necessarily sexual, and likely to lead to dangerous neuroses in the children as well as themselves. This attitude is reinforced by the natural laziness of adults where the understanding of children is concerned. It is convenient to have a supposedly scientific excuse for leaving the bother of one's offspring to others. Sex is so powerful a passion, so plainly animal in origin, and so delightful in experience, that it is not surprising that it has been vehemently marked down and over-emphasized by the ascetics as well as the rebels. What is more, it has become more intense in man than in the animals, through his more certain control of his food supply. I suggest however, that the parenthood or growth principle is of a less obvious but more compelling intensity, and that asceticism directed against it is likely to be as disastrous to the individual as sexual asceticism, and more disastrous to the society of which he is a member. In the individual who suppresses It one may observe an anger-reaction to the subject of children, which suggests a complex. And this growth principle—in a literal and not a mystical sense—is the animal or organic source of social co-operation. Like sex it must be intelligently manipulated, rather than destroyed or ignored. As yet this has never been attempted. Indeed, the tendency of modern organized states is more and more to ignore it together with all the other animal sources of our being.

The *reductio ad absurdum* of the confusion of the parental with the sex feeling is to be found in the patriarchal system, and especially in some of its modern exponents, such as Ludovici, who even goes so far as to maintain that the love of a mother for her young is a perversion of her sexual devotion to her mate induced by religious teaching. Missions have evidently been very effective among female cats, dogs, and other mammalian species. In the patriarchal system the male, as the source of the seed, arrogates to himself the right of property in the growth ; his desire to be immeasurably fat embraces not only a harem of several hundred wives, with their several hundreds of children, but the ox and the ass, the cattle and the crops reared and tended by his vaſt progeny. This attitude is indicative rather of the weakness than the ſtrength of the male's position. He has not the direct experience of ſteady creation by physical growth and travail of flesh and blood, which, physical suffering notwithſtanding, is so satisfying to the expansion impulses of the female ; therefore he requires ample and external reassurance of the fact that his ego is really expanding. This he seeks in ownership of wives, carefully imprisoned in taboos to ensure certain ownership of children. Indeed, the whole confusion between the parental and sexual impulses may be due to the dominance of male philosophy in all consideration of this subject. For the male, parental creation is intimately associated with the sexual moment ; he neither bears, nor in moſt cases, tends or educates the offspring. To the woman the sexual moment, though intensely desired and enjoyed for itself, is the mereſt incident in the satisfaction of the older impulse to gain power and abundant or eternal life by multiplying her own body. Feminists have recognized this fact, but, misled by sexual asceticism, they have made it the glory of virtuous women that they merely submitted to sex to obtain the children they desired. They carried this further and saw in the sexual submission of wife to husband symbolized by the acceptance of his name, a greater humiliation than the filial submission of all the children to the father and their acceptance of the paternal name. The perpetuation of the father's name is the most powerful instrument of male dominance. It is an instrument, not of sexual, but of parental inspiration. Equal guardianship of children is a step forward, but the patriarchal tyranny will not be broken until girls perpetuate the names of their mothers and boys only the names of their fathers. Some will urge that even this is reactionary : every new child born should have its own name unhampered by the name and tradition of either parent. This would, however, be parental asceticism in the sense described above, denying the very real link of animal growth and heredity. It would not be really fair to the children because, though they revolt from their parents, they have also a passionate desire to become parents themselves.

There are then two important irrational ingredients in parental feeling ; the first, the blind desire to expand and grow, to know that there exist in the world persons of our own flesh and blood ; and second, the intimate physical sympathy resulting from feeding and teaching the children when they are very young. The first is traditionally, though not necessarily, a masculine form, and the second traditionally, though not necessarily, a feminine form of the relationship. Both are entangled in a vast network of rationalizations connected with property, inheritance, economic support of husband for wife and children, and of children for parents in their declining years. In the closer knit organization of modern society, many of these economic sanctions are disappearing. They would disappear faster if the taboos handed down from the patriarchal system and medieval asceticism were not so deeply implanted. Thus there are to-day quite a number of fathers who are by no means the sole economic support of their children ; quite a number of women in a position to refuse the slavery of the old-fashioned marriage; quite a number of single women whose economic position would allow them to have and rear their own family of children, without a permanent husband. Social taboos, not economic difficulties, are the deterrent factor in these latter cases.

Many people have maintained that property is the sole basis of the family system, and that these economic changes will suffice to alter all our traditional ways of feeling. Clearly, the sexual jealousy of men and women is largely bound up with property. The man needs certainty of descent if he is to support his children and leave his property to them ; the woman clings to her right of financial support as wife and mother. There are quite a number of fathers who would take less interest in their children if they did not have to earn bread and butter for them. Equally there are parents who would lose interest in their children if they could not send them to sweated labour to swell the family income. None the less, the family stands for something more than an economic unit. Abolish property and inheritance, establish a matriarchy of endowed mothers, or give over all children at birth to State care and State support, and there will still be men and women who hunger to know which are their children, to help them, and to see them make their mark in the world. They do not yearn over them in misplaced sexual longing ; they simply feel this is me : as much a part of me as my hand, my eyes, or the vital organs of my body.

It is perfectly true that large numbers of modern people seem not to possess this feeling, or even to understand it in others. Where the patriarchal system survives strongly, either in fact or tradition, as among the Chinese or the Jews, parental feeling is more readily understood. But European and American people have a long period behind them in which racial immortality has been sublimated in the personal immortality of individual souls, and sex life brought into prominence by castigation. The natural result, in a society such as ours, where family ties are less and less essential to individual survival, is a crop of riotous individuals who, while willing to earn their own living, claim their right to the fullest personal freedom and personal experience that life can offer them. This, of course, implies complete sexual freedom, and, since they feel little or no impulse to self-perpetuation, a freedom from parental responsibility. The clue to this attitude is, I believe, that these people are deeply marked by the individualism of the Christian " soul ", and, having lost their faith in immortality hereafter, they seek the fullest experience on earth as a compensation. Except in so far as sex love can melt them, they remain themselves and within themselves for ever. Medieval Christianity bent these hard individual souls—for whose creation its own doctrine was responsible—by sacrifice and penitence to social co-operation ; modern theorists hope to achieve the same grudging result by economic organization.

Why then, if parental feeling in so many people is dying, and we can by economic organization provide for State feeding and State education of the children, should there be any reason for trying to keep parental feeling alive ? No reason at all, except that it is a powerful source of happiness both for parents and children ; and that this book treats, not of convenient and tidy systems, but of the endeavour to reach the fullest measure of human happiness. Economic organization has an important part to play, but it has very definite limits. It is possible to imagine a very well run State accepting all responsibility for the children, each parent continuing at his or her technical work, and men, women, and children exceedingly unhappy. The matriarchal solution might give instinctive happiness to mothers and children and involve much unhappiness for men. Maternity might be endowed, mutual fidelity no longer necessary, paternity quite unimportant and paternal feeling almost disappearing in large numbers of men. Women would easily find men to be the fathers of their children without further interest or responsibility, but those men who were strongly paternal might find themselves unable to be certain of children that were their own, or unable to obtain any right to more than the most casual relationship with them. What is needed for mutual happiness seems to be not a decline of paternal or a mere intensification of maternal feeling, but the fusion of the two in an individual and communal philosophy. If we are to admit rights of parents at all, then those rights must be for father and mother, if both desire them. If both do not then one or other is free. But we are forced to the conclusion that a compact to have children may involve very nearly a life-long partnership, though not by any means strict marital fidelity. It does, however, quite clearly mean an honourable limitation of freedom on the woman's side, sufficient to ensure the certainty of descent. A few years of agreed sexual fidelity seems the simplest method. Those whom that irks must find other ways that are both definite and honest. The almost complete certainty of contra-ceptives, when intelligently used, helps the solution of this problem.

We cannot resuscitate the patriarchal system : it is dying. We cannot put women back into the prison of economic dependence, nor men and women into the old iron cage of monogamy. But we have got to safeguard the economic and psychological interests of the children, who are, after all, the future of society. It becomes all the more urgent to define as clearly as possible the difference between sexual and parental partnerships.

Enforcement of the old family life by economic compulsion of fathers and mothers is not in the best interests of the children. It makes them still, what they have always been in fact and thought, a mere pendant to their parent's sexual desires. Marriage was, and still is, in the main a sexual compact, entered into because the man and woman concerned could, in the delicate phraseology of the ascetics, no longer restrain their carnal desires. So long as it remains the only respectable way out of that situation, and taboos forbid genuine sexual freedom, people will not be induced to think of marriage as a serious parental partnership. Gay and insistent sex will continue to overshadow its graver and lovelier companion. In America the sex basis of marriage has been more than ever emphasized, divorce has been made easy and respectable, and marriages are made and unmade for a passing fancy. It is wedlock, so children are permitted, but it rarely occurs to the couples concerned to wait and see if it lasts before they make themselves responsible for a child. In Colorado Judge Lindsey, in his *Revolt of Modern Youth*, computes that of the boys in a certain school, fifty per cent had fathers who had divorced, or been divorced by, the mothers. Children of such broken marriages do suffer, as society is at present constituted—perhaps they would always suffer—from the loss of the united parental care as a background to their early years. Whether or not the school is an efficient substitute will depend upon its personnel and the spirit in which it is organized. This is why it is so important to unearth and make active the old animal parental feeling wherever it is found, and, combining it with expert knowledge, turn it to the service of children, whether in parental partnerships, nursery, and other schools, or the Public Health services. Above all, let us set free from the burden of having and caring for children all those who do not possess it. Let men and women have as much sexual freedom as they desire, provided they will realize that the deliberate creation of children is a thing apart, involving probably a long period of mutual partnership, or the greatest possible care in bestowing and providing for the children.

As I see it, all men and women might find happiness in sex if they so desired and a large number in parenthood. All could work at any kind of work which suited them, but it would be preferable that most of those women who specially turned to maternity and those men in whom the paternal instinct was strong should be engaged in professions directly and indirectly bearing on the welfare of children. Such professions are nursery school work, teaching, doctoring, the supervision of food supply and to some extent housing. It is all very well to talk of expert care of children, but if it is to be done well our State institutions must be shot through and through with genuine and enlightened parental feeling. Instead of enclosing the genuine mother in the home, we have to bring her out to the service of the community. If, on the other hand, the exodus of the mothers means simply that they do a man's work in the world,[1] giving over their children almost from birth to the care of an army of trained spinsters, there may easily be a decline of love

[1] I do not mean that women with special aptitudes should give up their work when they become mothers. In a society which discarded the superstition of chastity, there would be plenty of mothers to spare after teaching, doctoring, etc., had been supplied.

for children in us all, and a misunderstanding of their rights and their place in the general scheme of happiness. This is happening now on a small scale and is likely to continue. One may instance the harshness of some landlords and employers to people with even moderate sized families. Even sublimated maternal instinct which is strong in simple types of single women is tending to disappear in the general process of desiccation which seems to be taking place. People in whom the parental and sex instincts are twisted and suppressed as they are in so many men and more especially in women, will not, whatever their expert training, have the stable calm and breadth of understanding which are essential to really good handling of children of all ages. The spirit of monasticism pervading our teaching system from the universities downwards, and the attempt to enforce celibacy on all women in the public health and other public services, is not only unjust, but actively inimical to the creation of a happy society. The spinster or ascetic type of moral and intellectual training is the source of so very many of our maladies and discontents.

Let us turn back from possible ideal organization to the present state of our society. Here is the deepest misery and confusion. Parenthood is anything but free, and anything but a spontaneous joy. Not only do we deny parenthood to people who desire it, but we make life hard for parents, and force children upon many people who would prefer not to have them at all.

Some men and women do not care at all for children, others, usually people of vitality, will say even in early youth that they would not like to feel they could never have a child. Think of this and then think once more of the women compelled in our society if not to complete chastity at least to childlessness. To have a child they must find a man for whom they are willing to sacrifice work and freedom for the remainder of their lives, and who in his turn must be willing to work for and support the wife and mother till he dies. Quite often a woman marries and is cheated, for the husband is a wastrel and she dares not embark on maternity because social customs do not permit her to work and support children. She is graciously permitted to go charing perhaps, though she may have been a teacher or skilled industrial worker. Why cannot every healthy woman who wants a child have one if she is willing to work to keep it ? Why can she not receive something from the State in recognition of important services ? So silly are the notions of old-fashioned people in England that they think a woman who has been lucky enough to trick a man into legal marriage is entitled, even if childless, to financial support for the rest of her days. The man may die young, the State pensions his able-bodied childless widow. Yet mothers of illegitimate babies may struggle and die and their children wander the world starved in mind and body. And here is the precious source of those who might staff our nursery-schools with love, intelligence, and devotion. Then there are the men and women who are ready for a life-long contract but must wait for marriage and therefore wait for children while their instincts grow blunt with disuse and their minds and bodies, which should be young to cope with the child's developing years, grow stiffer and older before the man's position is secure enough to take the risk. These young people are not selfish : they have a real sense of parenthood as a creative responsibility. We need not get into a moral frenzy over those who are well-to-do and idle and like pianos or motor-cars and lap-dogs better than babies. That is their pleasure : let them enjoy. Children of theirs would be spoilt little brats or wistful with neglect. Some moral frenzy perhaps may be expended on those hearty upper-class fellows and their barren wives, who like to see that state of ignorance and poverty in parents, which produces ten citizens in one room on nothing a week. Parenthood is a right and a pleasure to be exercised as a free choice by free men and women. It is not a duty into which all and sundry are to be driven by kicks and ignorance to the detriment of their own happiness and that of the unfortunate human beings they create. Nor is parenthood to be abandoned by men or women in obedience to inhumane marriage laws which will not set them free from unhappy or sterile unions. There may be willingness to forego where the sex union brings vital happiness to both, but there should be no compulsion. And even those who agree to marry on the understanding that there be no children, should be free to break that tie should the desire for parenthood stir them with longing.

All difficult cases apart, we must do something to take from parenthood the worry and anxiety that almost invariably beset it. Fathers and mothers who should be giving the most exact care to the structure of their children—by which I mean bodies and minds—are worried beyond measure over how to provide the next meal, how to find and pay for house room and warmth, how to pay for the necessary doctoring, how to give the child a chance in life, even how to acquire the scientific knowledge necessary to adjust the size of the family to economic capacity. All parents would worry, of course, whatever we did for them—that is part of the parental pleasure. But to worry in a loving instinctive way over a child's faults or disabilities is a very different thing from seeing an adored and possibly talented child perish before our eyes in mind and body for lack of the food or care vital to its being. That parents must sacrifice is no answer. They do it gladly. Any sacrifice whose results are seen in health or intelligence to the child is not a pain to the parent but a pleasure. There is no effort involved in giving. There are, I believe, large numbers of parents who would die in slow agony for the safety and well-being of their children and feel a greater ecstasy than the martyr going to the stake. For parental sacrifice has in it the comforting ingredient of egotism; though we die, the child—our flesh and blood—lives on—his eyes, his hair perhaps, his tricks of speech, his thoughts and impulses perpetuating in him and his children's children our individuality which we prize.

The child may run counter to all we most believe in, throw down, dig at its foundations, yet instinct holds fast to that in him which we have given him, that which is ourselves and neither he nor anyone can take away.

This intense desire for self-perpetuation is under-estimated in our traditional scheme of values and by many modern people. Obviously the Christian who believes in immortality for his own soul will care less about perpetuating its qualities in his children. God and not he makes the new human beings, the parents are no more than the instrument of His creation. Therefore clearly, parental activity involves no more than disciplining our children to virtue. God has His purpose with their destiny on earth and the ultimate destiny of their souls Roman Catholic opponents of birth control follow this out logically. According to them, disease and starvation are to take their toll of bodies, but the souls of the babies are immortal and go to their destined place. A decline in the belief in immortality and asceticism brings as in all activities the instinctive side of parenthood uppermost. It tends also to make the family rather than the individual the unit we seek to preserve. This is quite clear in such nations as the Chinese, to whom immortality is practically confined to living in the worship and reverence accorded to them after death by the descendants they have left behind. Modern people can revivify this feeling and supplement it by the inherited knowledge of science—looking to their sons and daughters not for worship but for carrying on and intensifying all that was best in their forefathers and steadily casting aside, perhaps even breeding out, what was ignominious and bad.

## SEX AND PARENTHOOD

In this way parental feeling leaves the restricted
field of the family and attaches itself to the
destiny of the whole human race. Left free
or guided by knowledge rather than doctrine,
it will not substitute tyranny of race destiny
for the tyranny of the family, a religion or
a State. It will not seek to produce uniformity
and docility but real individuals. Parents who
have knowledge and instinctive devotion realize
quite clearly that we work through individuals
and by individuals the race is built. They
perceive that they themselves, not an external
Power, are the creators of their children,
forming the bodily part of their structure first
by physical activity, then by feeding and care ;
and the mental part by the training and
environment they give them in early years,
and the facilities for learning they provide in
later education. It is here that women in their
maternal function can bring a real contribution to individual and social practice. Well
might Christianity dread their emancipation,
for they have it in their power to destroy the
foundations of that antagonism between mind
and matter on which the doctrine of sin has
been built. The necessary pre-occupation of

women in maternity with physical and instinctive activities gives them in a civilization that despises matter a subordinate position. When they emerge and scientific teaching has given them the power to observe, and to speak without humility and without regard to the traditional views which too often lead them astray, they will blow this ascetic nonsense sky-high. How can anyone of intelligence who has carried a child in her body, suckled it, fed and watched it through its early life, go on believing funny tales about original wickedness, the desire of the soul to escape the prison of the body, the unimportance of fragility and disease provided we are ever striving upward to spiritual perfection ? How can she believe either that maternity is horrid and coarse, or that it is a natural function not to make a fuss over and the more she works and starves herself the easier it will be ? What breath is wasted on sweet sentiment about maternity that should be saved for imparting unpalatable home truths. The more that mothers know and the more that they observe, the clearer it becomes that you can neglect nothing in this business. Heredity and the environment of both parents count, and the whole structure of the mother, her mental equipment, bodily health, and the kind and quantity of work she does during pregnancy, her diet, attention at childbirth and afterwards. Then the child : a creature of reflexes from which for good or evil in three or four years those who tend it will form a soul—a soul conditioned by and interwoven with its physical structure and customary physical and mental activities. Indeed, to be exact, not a soul at all nor destined for heaven, but a personality to play its part in the destiny of the world. Let women go into maternity with as much knowledge about the world as they are capable of assimilating—about everything, not only one province, since all knowledge is inter-connected ; let them be allowed complete sex freedom, be bred to courage and independence, and then give them power over feeding the community, over nursery schools as well as in every depart-ment of life. I believe that the creative delight of parenthood would be more and more realized by the whole community and that as we turned our attention more and more to the happiness of the child, so would our political institutions,

our foreign policy, our perspectives, our
dreams, our very natures be turned from
pursuing hatred and destruction to the delight
and happiness of conscious creation. I do not
write this as a pious sentiment nor as a vision
of the " little child " leading the lion and the
lamb to lie down in peace together. I record
it as a sober fact of human experience that
there is no activity so delightful, when conditions permit of its exercise without undue
toil and anxiety, and when we approach it
without a lot of prejudices against slavery
and " women's work ", as mutual co-operation between men and women over the care
and education of babies and young children.
Men unhampered by masculine pride and
dignity and women without foolish delicacy
or feminist bias find all the arduous and
trifling activities involved in this task both
exciting and delicious. When the child
runs in the sunshine or looks up with an
intelligent question there stirs in the nature of
both parents that bedrock emotion of parental
pride—this alert mind—these bright limbs
we have made, we ourselves, and shall tend
and nurture till we die. That we have made

the child is no more than the simple truth ; that our laws and policy can give happiness and scope to that living personality or darken and put out in it the lamp of creation is equally simple and equally true. Yet very few perceive this. If they were many, child culture would be the pivot of our civilization round which would revolve the greater part of human activity. Deep and real co-operation in parenthood between men and liberated women could regenerate society. With his customary superiority man has classed women with children. Close upon the heels of woman's emancipation follows the emancipation of the child.

## V

### THE RIGHTS OF CHILDREN

So far we have dealt with the world as we find it, a medley of men and women holding all sorts of antiquated beliefs and driven hither and thither by instincts which they neither understand nor recognize and therefore thwart in countless ways. All these people have in my view a right to happiness, and we cannot therefore baulk them of the profound instinctive desire to perpetuate their beliefs and way of life in their children. However misguided some parents may think other parents, they have not the right to interfere whether as individuals or legislators between parents and children. Obviously this is allowable in extreme cases, where the parents are devoid of love and show cruelty and neglect. But where they are doing the best they can according to their mental development the battle for freedom is a task for the children themselves.

The legislator can only help by setting limits to parental power after the children reach a certain age, and by requiring a sufficient degree of knowledge to make the child capable of independence through work. This may seem a hard saying, for parents are notorious reactionaries where their children are concerned. But if anybody—and clearly somebody must— is to have rights of property in children in their early years—it is on the whole preferable that the parents, rather than the State or Church, should have those rights. Where parental feeling exists at all, it will produce in the sternest men and women a watchful kind of love which a child can get from nobody else in quite the same measure, and the unattractive child whom nobody else loves or understands may be saved from utter despair by parental tenderness. I prefer to rely on the propaganda of enlightened people to educate the parental instinct rather than on repressing it or producing artificial substitutes. I rely also on allowing those people who really dislike children to be set free from the burden of having them. The same principle applies here as in dealing with sex : to leave but little room for tyranny and a great deal for education. We may assume in normal people who have chosen parenthood a genuine desire for the well-being of their children. We must work through this, not against it. The more that people come to know of science the more will they look upon parenthood as a creative activity directed to new achievements rather than to conserving the past. They will not desire for their children just the same education as they themselves received but rather the best that modern skill can provide. Parental happiness has the great merit of continuing on into old age when other pleasures are diminishing. For the enlightened parent this pleasure is intensified, by watching with passionate interest rather than with malevolence the changes which his offspring make in their way of life and the government of the world.

Some may think that the education of parents is too slow a method of achieving children's rights and that swift action by the State and its experts would be preferable. This is the line taken in modern Russia and to a lesser degree in all modern nations. But current emotion about nationalism and State worship should make us cautious. We have not only to deny that the child is a servant of God, but that he is the servant of a nation. The child is subordinate to no abstract principle, he is the future of humanity. Strictly speaking, no person who believes that wars between classes and nations are inevitable is fit to be in charge of the destiny of children. To believe in the unity of the human race and get children to believe it in early youth would mean the creation of that unity and the end of war. The present holders of power and nearly all the candidates for power in most countries are unfit to be trusted with our children. Parents do sometimes care if their children live or die, they are sometimes sorry if they are killed in battle, but the rulers of States educate and prepare their human material for starvation, slavery, and slaughter. Some might think that this only applies in States where old-fashioned education prevails, or at any rate among people unacquainted with modern psychological methods. To read an American compilation, *The Child, His Nature, and His Needs*, would open their eyes. In this book a series of chapters containing very modern psychological and medical study is concluded by bare-faced advice on the teaching of 100 per cent nationalism, and a plea for all the year round schools on the ground that commercial rivals will outstrip a country that is behind in education. " The wars hereafter," we are told, " will probably be fought more largely in the schoolrooms than on the battle-fields of the world." Whether or no this means that education is a preparation for soldiering, it is clear that those responsible for this compilation cannot lift their heads above national pugnacity as an ideal. Further, their account of how military examination revealed the poor state of national health throws a sinister light upon their deep concern for medical care of babies and young children. It is a grim picture—the wealth and power of modern educational science in the hands of these ungenerous, loveless, efficiency mongers, for one cannot but feel these defects in the attitude of some Americans to children. The clue to such defects is to be found, I firmly believe, in two chapters in the same book on sex and the differentiation of play instincts in boys and girls. These put forth the familiar old stuff referred to in my last chapter, and are variations on the old rhyme which tells us that girls are " sugar and spice and all that's nice " and boys " frogs and snails and puppy dog's tails ". If they are representative of American schools and parents, as I believe they are, they go to show that from early youth the American boy is being wantonly suggested into a he-man, the girl into the ancient dishonesty of the delicate female, whatever the outward camouflage of athletic boyishness, camaraderie, and respect for feminist rights. There is in America a greater lack of understanding of sex-love and instinctive parental feeling than even in England. Yet these are the mainspring of generosity and creativeness. Where sex is choked and mishandled education will continue to be, even with modern methods, a dry national tyranny and in no sense a contribution to world civilization. There is just one hope of a State which, like America, goes so far as to nurture the creative impulses of the very young. It is that the young, by virtue of their early education, will refuse to conform to the last taboos of sex and patriotism, which their short-sighted elders still struggle with might and main to bind about their growing minds.

That said, let us temporarily forget old-fashioned forms of education and assume that our mothers and fathers have the quickened instincts and scientific intelligence necessary to the important work of creating a modern child. We are now desirous, not of perpetuating ancient tradition but of making new human creatures. We have to consider the environment in which they are to live, the work they will have to do, the beliefs which it is advisable they should entertain. If we want the best of our children, we have to find out all that science can teach us about the formation and growth of their bodies, about diet, and possible defects, and most important of all what it can teach about psychology and early education. If we are not able to learn and apply such knowledge, but none the less believe in modern views of life, we shall of course give the care of our children to people who are expert. It cannot be too much emphasized that to produce and rear a child from the day of conception onwards until it reaches adult life is work which requires expert skill and expert knowledge, and those people who are not prepared to equip themselves in the necessary way must either abandon parenthood or have recourse to the expert. Every woman intending maternity must know all she is capable of knowing about conception, contraception, pregnancy, childbirth, and breast feeding. If she is going to tend the children herself or supervise this work, she must know a great deal more. If she does not, both she and the father must learn, what is often a hard lesson, to accept the influence that nurses and teachers will have upon their offspring. The nurse, nursery school or teacher must be chosen with the greatest care, and ignorant parents in all classes of life learn to forego interference. Here again, there must not be compulsion. Those who run crèches, hospitals, schools, are apt to forget the primary rights of even the most foolish of parents. Knowing what is best for the child they tend to command rather than instruct those who have given it life. Ignorance is not a crime in parents who have had no opportunity of learning. Therefore free lectures for those who are to be fathers and mothers should be part of the educational activity of all local authorities. It is appalling that we still do so little to diminish the ignorance of the enormous number of people who are producing and rearing little children without the first notion as to what it is all about. Every day you can meet them in public places nagging or spoiling, laying the foundations of incompetent bodies and dull and incompetent minds. The psychological principles which establish confidence and harmony between a parent and a young child are not difficult to understand, nor are they difficult to carry out even by hardworking fathers and mothers, provided they do not have a torrent of young children. Yet usually the child, which is a potential personality, is first of all treated as a toy and afterwards, when it has developed the manners appropriate to such treatment, it becomes a horrid little nuisance, that mother or father, whoever happens to be sternest, must take in hand for discipline.

What we have to remember first of all is the child's right to be happy. The parent must help it to this achievement as a baby, as a child, and as an adult. This does not mean always giving a child the thing it cries for at each particular moment. Nothing could be worse than that, except to deny it everything in which it seems to take pleasure. When people reacted from severe notions of child education, they at first thought that the aim of parents and teachers should be to give free play to the nature and personality said to be born in each child. This view is still too much held. In actual fact a child at birth has no "nature" in that sense, it is a structure which develops instincts and desires in response to the stimulus of environment. The activities it requires are rigidly appropriate to the needs of its growth and the similarity in behaviour between two healthy children of identical age is astonishing. The child is a human being according to the definition I have given, for it desires food, activity, and knowledge. Its sex feelings develop also but less early, I think, than Freudians maintain. We have to know all stages of growth and the treatment appropriate to each. The kind of food and play that are necessary will constantly change, nor can a child assimilate all kinds of knowledge at each stage. A tiny baby cannot even focus its eyes or judge distance and shapes of objects. Nor can it control at will any muscular movement except possibly sucking. A human being has to learn absolutely everything, from digestion to the higher branches of mathematics. We must think of a child not as mind and body, but as a structure capable of displaying what we call mental and physical types of activity. Our early care must be devoted to seeing that the faculties which it will use develop unimpaired either by overstrain, lack of use or disease. Given a normal healthy infant it is the fault of those who care for it if, barring serious accidents, it grows up with a bad digestion, weak bones, poor muscles, bad eyes, bad teeth, a mis-shapen body. As we come to know more, I believe we shall find that nearly all stupidity is also due to wrong feeding and handling and unintelligent environment in early youth. It is already, I think, quite certain that most moral defects arise from early misdirection or thwarting of emotions.

Our child then must become a perfect physical instrument. Obviously I cannot here enter into detail on this aspect of the question. The best medical men and women of our time are now doing all they can to spread the necessary knowledge through hand-books and welfare centres. But they still neglect too much the province of psychology, which is not only vital to character and intelligence but reacts upon the health and shape of the body. It is well known that a child may display a lazy mind and develop a stoop because its eyes are defective, but conversely, perpetual snubbing or rough treatment may cause it to hang its head and walk with a slouch or develop nervous tricks that are very difficult to cure. Children must be given an attitude of mind which leads them to face the universe with open friendliness and courage, then they will walk with upright heads, springing feet and alert and eager eyes. Similarly, abounding health and vitality will predispose a child to happy activities, and in more subtle ways the chemical nature of its blood and the action of its glands will in the main determine temperament and size.[1] This chemical action in its turn is

[1] Intelligence also, as the discoveries about thyroid glands show.

conditioned, it may be, as much by early feeding and environment as by inherited constitution.

When we are feeding or training a young child our aim should be not to impose upon it our standards of taste and behaviour, but to help it through instinct first to maintain its growing body and then to obtain familiarity with, and power over its environment. A very young baby that is always played with and amused when it cries will be slow to learn the spontaneous kicking and crowing by which it develops its muscles and sets forth on the road to individual activity. If it is not ill, to cope with its legs and its lungs is its natural pleasure, an assertion of its right to happy activity that the adult corrupts by unnecessary intervention. Take another simple example from the hunger instinct. Future happiness demands that a young child should have regular meal times, but otherwise natural hunger should determine all our feeding of children. When hungry they will eat anything, therefore good food and the right kind for their needs must then be set before them. Instinct teaches them quite rightly to use food to maintain the body and not as a major pleasure. When the child is not hungry, sweetening and seasoning and tempting with grown-up food merely corrupts its simple pleasures and lays the foundation of greed and fastidiousness which may have harmful results for happiness in later life. I think healthy children like the food which is good for them. Grown-up food, of course, has prestige, because grand people like grown-ups eat it. But it should not be given, even in scraps for a treat. A child readily understands if it never receives it that it is not appropriate to its needs. It does not aspire to eat grass and hay because it knows quite well that it will not grow into a cow or a horse. Grown-up prestige should be sparingly applied in certain directions. For this reason it is good for children to have their own meal-times and eat in company with each other. The nursery school where all young children eat and help to serve one another is the best means to their health and happiness. It is more democratic than a family because the child meets many others of its own age and acquires an immediate and natural feeling of independence. Children slightly older stimulate its ambition in habits and play, but it finds big children and many grown-ups merely stupid and a nuisance. The parent who bullies or coaxes a child that will not eat is not only probably destroying its digestion, but certainly creating an exacting tyrant or a neurotic. Similar principles apply to learning the habit of healthy and regular sleep. I have seen well-handled and happy children put to bed in broad daylight snuggle down with a sigh of exquisite pleasure and smile themselves off to sleep not so much like a healthy adult after a real day's work, as a sybarite lulled on a silken couch by rare and beautiful music.

The sensuous pleasures of healthy children are intense beyond anything adults know, unless it be the pleasures of love. The texture and taste of food, colour and texture of materials, sizes, and shapes, movements of plants and trees in the wind, animals moving, and the movements of their own bodies, including rest after excited activity, fill them with astonishing ecstasy and delight. It is so easy, and so cruel, to blunt their delicate senses and instincts by inappropriate food, habits, and play and thus twist their capacity for enjoyment in later years. A child is so new, it can be got to enjoy anything. It is so much at the mercy of adult suggestion. That being so we should use this power, which comes to us whether we will or no, to draw out in the child everything that makes for happiness and creative effort now and in later life. I have no patience with people who say that human equality is nonsense and that equality of opportunity is all that a social system need provide. Inheritance of qualities and defects is undeniable, but very early environment does more to destroy or intensify qualities and defects than people are willing to realize. To realize this is inconvenient, because we should then have to interpret equality of opportunity as a right of every child—and its mother before its birth—to sufficient really good food, medical care, and healthy and intelligent surroundings. Equality would have to begin not in competing in the labour market, but at birth. So in fact it should and until it does, we have no right to consider that we are a civilized people. " Men are *born* free and equal " wrote Rousseau. Yet the chains of poverty, serfdom, ignorance that encircle their fathers and mothers twine about baby limbs and baby minds from the hour of birth. Apart from economic and social disabilities parents hand on by suggestion age-old fears, repressions and evil lusts which they ought to be ashamed of communicating to their free-born children, who are the heirs of science, masters of the world, beings in whom the fire of creative thought is burning and may flame out in splendours and triumphs none of us can foretell. What we do know is this. That we can do our part to set them free from things that have enslaved us in our generation ; give them enough and right food, help them to cast out fear, to scorn ignorance, to defeat disease, to value instinctive happiness for themselves and others, and to go out equipped with a courage and a personality shaped for creativeness to meet and surmount the difficulties and dangers that will beset them in their time. When they are grown, we can stand aside (though we long to protect them), glorying in them when they reach their desired achievements, and—if we may or can—comforting them when they fail.

This function of a quiet background—source

of knowledge and security—should be begun by the parent while the child is very young. When it can walk and talk it begins to educate itself in all kinds of activities. It likes to run and jump in childish ways, but it also likes to practise what is done by grown-ups and older children. It will construct castles and trains and railways, stamping with rage and despair when inert matter refuses to obey its orders. It will imitate exactly the motions of people scrubbing and dusting, mixing mortar, laying bricks, driving motor-cars. Then is the time to lead it away from hatred and destruction to the greater pleasures of creative effort. Parents and nurses too often do the contrary, deliberately calling out destructive pleasure by building the child castles to destroy and letting it tear flowers to pieces. Yet the child enjoys much more building for itself and sowing and watering its own seeds and plants. When a child hurts itself or cannot make its toys obey people call unoffending tables and chairs or bricks or puffers " naughty ", thus giving the child a sense of injured innocence instead of letting it feel its own silliness and incompetence. Or else they encourage false sentiment by saying " poor chair ", or " poor table ". This may seem a very trifling matter, but in actual fact such misdirection lays the foundation of a superstitious attitude to the outside world. This is, in savages, the basis of religion. Then again people teach children to give toys to other children (especially the poor) or share them with friends in a spirit of condescending charity instead of an obvious and natural partnership in pleasure with their fellow creatures. The wrath of the gods, in the shape not of slaps but of an angry reproof rarely used, should descend upon a child who pushes or strikes another intentionally. No mercy should be shown in this respect even to quite tiny children. Here again I think many people make a mistake in telling the other child to stand up for itself and setting one child against the other. Rivalry plays a quite natural part in education and should never be artificially stimulated, especially in early years. It is astonishing how quickly a young child can learn that deliberately to hurt a sentient creature or override the rights of another is a crime it must never commit. Hurting in competitive games comes later when the child is quite able to understand that the odds are equal and the contest fair because according to definite rules. Personally I am not sure how far sports that involve hurting human beings or live creatures even with " fair play ", should be used in training for courage and endurance. I prefer on the whole to pit them against the forces of nature in rowing, swimming, and diving, or climbing, and against each other in running and jumping. For physical grace and health eurythmics, acting, and dancing are superior to sport in that they unconsciously stimulate a harmony of mind and body. This harmony is left out of traditional English education because we still educate either body or mind separately. As in medieval times, we had the education of the knightly warrior and the learned clerk, so to-day we have the public school athlete and the intellectual.

In all early education never tell the child or let it guess that you have a moral purpose. Do not preach it little sermons about how much better it is to create than destroy, to do good rather than evil. Stimulate it to constructive activities and let it find its own pleasure. The object is not to produce a set human being who works according to a consistent moral plan, but a line or chain of spontaneous, beautiful, and creative actions. The child that does not go to a nursery school can enjoy a great many of the same advantages if the parents are wise. The habit of enjoying concentrated work can be acquired at the age of three and even earlier. A child that sees mother and perhaps father, busy or working at stated times speedily asserts its right to " be busy " too, or will do so with the slightest suggestion. With its own table or chair in a corner—outdoors if possible, and clay, bricks, chalks, and paper, or a duster and small broom, it will work assiduously for a couple of hours with but little help and stimulus from adults. Give it praise for the results it achieves in this way— not too much or too little. Do not praise it for eating and drinking or performing other bodily functions, except for improvements in self-help and cleanliness in all these respects.

On fear and on knowledge volumes might be written. Very nearly all the fears of children are inspired by the stupid timidity of adults. Never display fear before a child however much you may be feeling. They do not naturally fear the dark, or animals. They have a certain instinctive recoil from things that are unfamiliar which may easily become fear if it is encouraged. Nothing is so important in education as to reduce fear to a minimum. Mothers too often like the clinging dependence of babies, though they should be constantly taking pains to educate it away. A child unaccustomed to seeing people will draw back from a stranger and the foolish parent comforts it : " Did the big man frighten you then "—and so on ; or else rebukes it so sharply that what was merely hesitation at once becomes fixed as timidity. I saw a father on a steep and dangerous cliff once with a young child in his arms. The child was town-bred and cried with terror at the precipice and the wild sea below. The father was shaking it and saying—" If you don't shut up this minute, I shall throw you down." To say the same thing to him is the first impulse of a child-lover.[1] A little familiarity with steep places would have soon abolished that child's fears. Probably with

[1] Another child I observed was threatened with punishment for galloping up and down and tossing its head like a horse. When it grows up stupid its parent will be surprised.

different educators it would never have felt them, for a fear of steep places is unusual in children. But nothing predisposes to general timidity like an atmosphere of threats and bullying. Let your children become familiar with everything that at first seems strange to it. Let it handle frogs and snails and beetles if it will do so. Curb your anxiety when it approaches strange dogs. If it show timidity curb your own and handle strange beasts and insects yourself in its presence. When the child begins to jump and climb, do not forbid it but teach it the heights and places you know to be within its capacity. When it becomes necessary to restrain the child from rashness, it will then have confidence in your judgment and yet not exaggerate your prohibition into an irrational fear. When fear of anything develops never rest content until you have helped the child to conquer it. There must not be nagging or terrifying the child, but explanation as to the nature of the object—or movement— (sometimes they fear shadows and mechanical toys) which it dreads. Then follow with a gradually increasing familiarity with its presence and mechanism. To know the cause of a dreaded phenomenon is both with adults and children the most important step in conquering fear. Success in conquering fears by education is indubitable. I have seen a three-year-old child which shook and went pale with terror when taken within twenty yards of the sea so develop by careful education that after three months it leapt from a high sand castle into a rough wave that swept right over its head. When picked up though not completely cheerful, it did not cry, but inquired as a matter of scientific interest, " What did the sea do to me ? "—and turned and ran through the water back to the sand castle again.

The connection between the conquest of fear and the child's right to happiness is obvious. Observation of children or of one's own psychology shows that in the very act of conquering there is a release of relief and joy which sheds happiness for several hours and is the foundation of future enjoyment. Timidity breeds anxiety, incompetence, superstition, all of which are destructive to happy activity whether mental or physical. A human being bred to timidity dares not take responsibility or important decisions. In this way people often fail to grasp the one important adventure of their lives—in work or love—which would have brought full blossoming and fruiting to their nature. Every conquest of fear puts us more at ease in our environment, releases what is positive in our activity and diminishes the activities dictated by negative considerations. Who fears the sea cannot navigate it : who fears to live fully is already half-way to the grave. Worse still, he will be an impediment and a source of hatred and destruction among his fellow-men.

Some people regard emphasis on courage as dangerous, because they believe brute courage is the source of war and oppression and that timidity makes men gentle. There is some truth in this argument. It is not sheer brute courage which I have in mind, but a steadfastness built upon experience and wedded to sensitiveness. Very great numbers of our insensitive strong men are really cowards. Panic makes them fight, where courage would have made them think.

But let us not think fear is dead when it is only conquered by discipline. Destroying

**fear** and imparting knowledge are intertwined in education. The child repeats in this way the history of the race. He cannot learn if he is afraid, nor will he finally overcome fear and the rage which accompanies it except by science. Nearly all parents realize nowadays that they must answer a child's questions truthfully, or if they do not know the answers try and send him to somebody who does. Young children rarely forget any piece of knowledge that has come in answer to a question unless it is too difficult for them to grasp at that particular stage. A child of three whose questions have been patiently answered knows more about the sun and stars, the direction of the winds, the seasons, the behaviour of plants, animals and machines than many a badly educated adult. Environment stimulates questions, and one cannot attach too much importance to varied environment in early years. I think that to create a complete modern person, we must bear in mind that two activities are of fundamental importance to our society, the practice of agriculture and the practice of industry. Every child should feel these two forces in the marrow of his bones. At present some children live in towns and others in the country, to the great detriment of their harmonious development. What delights the town child misses—the plunge into blue sea-water, blackberrying on warm September days, watching the cows at milking, the fishermen mending their nets. What a misfortune also is the life of the upper-class child apart from knowledge of machines and factories which are romantic and wonderful to him in ways that might be fruitful for the improvement of industrial processes and conditions in later years. A child ought to know as if by feeling it the growth of crops, the breeding of animals and human beings, the movement of tides, winds and stars, the colours and habits of flowers and trees. It ought to know also the speed and manner of mechanical activity, processes of manufacture, chemistry, dynamics. We scarcely realize that when we run and jump on a bus or moving train we are exercising a faculty due to familiarity with environment; watch a peasant from a remote district in China try to do this, and you will speedily see that it is so. Moreover, a community of people quite unfamiliar with machines ill-treat them so that they become stubborn like badly managed horses. This feeling of familiarity with all types of activity prepares the way for exact learning about physics, biology, chemistry, medicine. The study of human anatomy and psychology, which is of first-class importance, can also begin quite early. A child can understand that people get tired and angry, and when anger is justifiable and when otherwise. It observes closely what its parents and other children enjoy, what they dislike and how they behave to other human beings. Helped by their behaviour, and their teaching, both apparent and concealed, it could be by the time it reaches school age a creature completely and securely at home in its relations to human beings, animals, mechanism, the weather, the sea, the earth, and the sky. I feel that this is what we want to produce: a creature that understands the texture and habits of its world so completely, that when exact science is added it will manipulate that world with the sureness and grace of the artist or the dancer who performs with easy abandon the most difficult of movements. The religious person would say that such education produces a nature at the level of the animals, or a soulless materialist, the romantic perhaps that it would neglect or extinguish divine inspiration. Such criticisms are really meaningless. If I cannot make clear to all but the bigoted the importance of getting behind the soul and body division I shall have written in vain. At birth we are simply a structure capable of receiving and assimilating food, drink, and impressions from the outer world. As our arms and legs grow, so do our imagination and intellect. The limbs feed upon food, the mind is made by impressions and habits. To impart fear to a child is like giving it poisonous food. If we try to think of a human being not as a rigid lump of matter directed by a spiritual force within, but rather as something yielding and swaying in its environment like sea-weed or the bodies of swimmers in the motion of the sea, we shall come nearer the truth. The mind and the more complex instincts are built out of early environmental influences. Therefore the more you enrich a child's nature with sense impressions and information—provided you do not overtax its strength—the more soul and imagination it will have. You are not writing on a clean slate so much as weaving a fabric. One impression interlocks with another to form an association, and these associations or complexes of thought and emotion become the imagination and the character of the adult. Vividness of impressions does much to determine character, and vividness depends, I believe, a great deal upon the bodily organs or the state of health when impressions are received. The accidents of life, weather, health, changes, the order in which impressions come, are different for each individual, even where the environment seems identical, and therefore no two personalities are exactly alike. It will be seen that the education of discipline and denial is not only trivial and superficial, but actually likely to produce more soulless materialists than an education based on scientific psychology. The soul which is an empty chamber, swept and garnished and pure, or filled with spiritual dreams and negative precepts that ignore the nature of the ravening material universe without, is not, as the religious think, an impregnable citadel. At the first onslaught it will fall to instinct, or to knowledge that destroys superstition, and will be more dominated by its animal nature than the personality which has been from the beginning interwoven with the texture of the universe, and therefore possesses instincts that play easily, like the supple fibres of well-nourished and well-practised muscles. If you build a dam the waters will break it with floods of destruction, if you make channels and water-courses the same springs will carry abundant loveliness to your fruits and flowers.

To religious people the epic of life unfolded in evolution is debasing. They dislike large-scale production and prefer to step new-made if not in body, at least in soul, from the hands of God. Little do they realize how strong an argument the souls that claim this source are to the promoters of atheism. At present the right to withdraw a child from denominational instruction is conceded to parents of unorthodox views. Similarly I would concede to the religious the right to prevent their children, when under age, from learning about evolution. Nay, more, should we not encourage this devout tendency and extend the embargo on science to doctoring and engineering? Surely the religious soul should seek no escape from the curse of Adam, but rather contribute humbly to communal needs by digging, hewing, drawing water, and the practice of those handicrafts which were in vogue when the Founder walked the earth. I would also extend the rights of the free-thinker and say that his children need not even learn the eighteenth century superstition of God the First Cause if he does not desire it.[1] They should be free not only of denominational teaching, but of all religion. They should read the Bible as racial chronicles, at a suitable age. Step by step, as they could understand it, they should be taught all that scientists know of the physical universe, and of the nature of man, not as dogma, but as a basis for further investigation. But what if all our boasted knowledge is false and vain ? Even if evolution is no more than a fable it is a better fable than Christianity. To hasten through a miserable world with closed eyes and deaf ears, saving our own souls and snatching up a few others as we pass, is a

---

[1] *The* (London) *Times,* discussing the Tennessee trial, winds up a solemn leader by suggesting that possibly the teaching of material or atomic origins of life should be discouraged and the Divine origin of creation taught as a basis of science.

233

poor dream of human existence. A scientific background of thought gives less selfishness, greater courage, wider horizons. To study life and know that its forms are constantly changing is to realize that we can ourselves, perhaps even consciously, contribute to variety and improvement. To look to an immortality expressed in terms of life in the universe to which our own life contributes is a wider view than concern for our own miserable survival. Christian sacrifice is forced, the devotion that arises from a scientific philosophy is natural and easy. In evolution, chemistry, dynamics, physics, anatomy, we see ourselves linked naturally to the universe in which we live, yet by no means enslaved to it. This is an incentive to effort, to expansion, to acquiring knowledge. Instead of becoming hollow shells of virtue, we employ all our faculties, we learn, do, and enjoy all that we can, finally laying down our lives content in the thought that our human structure at least has contributed something to the intricate life of the world. So may a plant perish that has been perfect in leaf, blossom, and fruit and in the seedlings that spring about its roots as it withers, so may the parent perish who has given his best to his children, so may the lover, the poet, the artist, the engineer, the farmer, the teacher, and all mortal men and women who have known, however faintly, the breath of creation, go down into the grave in security and peace.

Is science to be the sole background of modern education, and will the arts perish as no more than pursuits of racial childhood? I have not space here to argue at length on what I believe to be a stupid and artificial rivalry between science and art. Our notion of science is still dominated by the mechanical physics we derive from Newton, our notions of art by aristocratic traditions and old-fashioned psychology. Art that means anything in the life of a community must bear some relation to current interpretations of the mystery of the universe. Our rigid separation of the humanities and the sciences has temporarily left our art stranded or stammering and incoherent. Both art and science ought to be blended in our early education of children's emotions and powers of observation, and that harmony carried forward in later education. The imagination and practice of the scientist and artist are not so far apart as most of us think. Moreover, in their attitude to matter both are the enemies of ascetic religion. I cannot agree with Shaw's *Methuselah* that art can interpret only the same childish themes again and again. His work and that of Wells is evidence to the contrary. In both these men knowledge of current science and the emotions of the artist have blended to help construct the new philosophy so needed in our time.

The importance of artistic expression through music, dancing, acting, and painting is likely to be under-estimated by modern educationists in industrial countries such as America. Industrial mechanism and behaviourist psychology have together suggested what is called the dynamic method of education in which all education is externalized and made real by practical handling of matter. This is already inherent in the Montessori method for young children with its apparatus and discouragement of day-dreams and fancies.[1] Dynamic education, which allows free movement and experiment for children, is contrasted

[1] I think this all very sound as regards early teaching except that free fancy has its place.

with old European methods of book-learning and sitting still in class. It is perfectly true that European teaching suffers from the influence of monastic contemplation and does not establish the obvious correlation between contemplation and the visual or tactile sensations and memories which are its source. But equally dynamic education ignores the fact that mind and imagination are quite early composed as faculties which can and should be exercised whole as well as in their component parts. It is just by sitting still and getting free of direct contact with the material world and arranging images and memories in new series of patterns that the artist creates and the scientist makes his discoveries. Each then, unlike the religious, returns to test the value of his imaginings through the senses. Therefore, though to live entirely in a world of fairy tales and fancies is mistaken, it is equally mistaken to live entirely in a world of counting beads and measuring jars. A child must learn to carry numbers, quantities, shapes, colours, sounds, within himself as images and to combine them and put them forth without perpetual relation to the things they represent.

Only by this method are new thoughts and new images born. More than that it has an important effect in imaginative sympathy with other people. Of a child educated purely by dynamic methods I would expect restlessness, lack of co-ordination when undirected, a glib mechanical capacity to pass intelligence tests, but little originality or breadth of vision. He will do for a mechanical, but not a human society. Artistic expression in which the limbs and muscles put forth the dreams of the inner life, either in motion, colour or sound, or all these combined, is the right counterpart to education by experiment, in which the outward sensations manufacture the images of the mind.

To sum up, then, what a modern parent may desire for children. First of all the health which gives the vitality and beauty on which all their functions will be built ; next an early training that will call out in them friendliness, courage in thought and action, sensitiveness to love, to beauty, and the happiness of others; and a life which, by providing few but right outlets for fear and its correlative rage, will lead to the easy abandonment of the baser passions.

Finally that their minds be filled with the visions of scientific and artistic achievement, inspired and tuned to understanding of human life by literature and poetry. Once their character has taken shape, let them know all that man is capable of, not only his heroisms, but his crimes, hypocrisies, his pitiful follies. Let there be no Achilles' heel of ignorance and repression through which lust for wealth or power or cruelty may enter to poison and corrupt the personality. So equipped, so armed, so adorned, pennants flying, sails swelling, bows lifting in eager pride, they glide to the launching, they the ark of our deliverance, the argosy of our adventure. Breathless in heart and body with the effort of creation, trembling with hope for their achievement and fear of their disaster, we watch, till life and vision fail us, their gallant progress towards the uncharted seas.

# VI

## Modern Civilization

The reader who has passed hastily, as readers will, over the preceding chapters, will exclaim that there is nothing new in the discovery of human instinct and the claim that a life lived according to our nature so revealed, may bring us happiness. What is the use of re-stating a Rousseauistic hedonism which has been tried and found to lead in individuals and in communities to confusion and disaster? Remove the restraint of religious morals, corsets, even clothes, and the life of men and women is seen to be as Hobbes saw it, so " nasty and brutish " that its shortness is its sole redeeming feature. If human beings are not bullied and repressed, they will merely eat and drink, be merry, idle, and cruel to the end of their days. I would freely admit that this is true of many people, especially of those now called virtuous. What I do not admit is that a frank abandonment to pagan voluptuousness is in any degree more wicked than a life of personal repression which, under cover of hypocritical abstractions such as religion, empire, patriotism, scientific organization, moral uplift, exercises on a grand scale the evil passions which in the simple animal only bring suffering to himself and a few others of his species. Organized murder and cruelty are in no way preferable to the ravenings of individuals despite the cunning device of a flag, a shibboleth, incense, an altar, to make them seem so. Animals we are, and animals we remain, and the path to our regeneration and happiness, if there be such a path, lies through our animal nature. Therefore, when we have been at great pains to drag one uncomfortable corset off our bodies, we should be slow to imprison them in another, however alluring its supple grace and hygienic properties as depicted in the advertisements. I am not impressed by external devices for the preservation of virtue in men or women. Marriage laws, the police, armies and navies are the mark of human incompetence. We have not yet found the right road to conquering ourselves and our environment. If we cannot move forward to creating human beings who can be safely let loose among their fellow creatures to enjoy and do good rather than harm, then our life is vain and we may as well all perish on the field of Armageddon.

The instinctive nature of man is not desperately wicked nor supremely virtuous. It is not unchanging, but neither is it so malleable that we can treat it with violence or contempt. The conservative who is imprisoned in his notion that instinct is so wicked that it cannot be dealt with except by repressive laws, is at least not so foolish as to think that it is not there. He recognizes cowardice and greed, which bring militarism and private property in their train. What he does not choose to perceive is how a society built on his particular abstractions, religion and patriotism, reinforces the destructive instincts and stifles the creative ones.[1] The modern reformer sees quite clearly that there is much in our social system which makes men and women wicked, but is very

[1] The *Times* contribution to a recent discussion on industrial psychology was the blunt suggestion of utilizing greed and rivalry in piece-work and competition to enrich the employers by greater production. This is the reality in a society whose religion professes to make men noble and virtuous.

prone to the view that to destroy the system will make everybody virtuous. When, as in Bolshevik Russia, this theory is seen to be fallacious, he hurriedly seizes a new strait-jacket and claps it on society. It is a common-place argument against socialists, but a com-pletely valid one, that when young, eager and penniless they are possessed of idealistic beliefs in human nature, but that when they become rich, or when they marry and have children, they forget all that nonsense and become ordinary grasping members of a competitive society. Sometimes to avoid this result such people impose on themselves an abstinence like that of Christians. Though not chaste, they will love no one deeply for fear of the snares of affection, they will not have children because they observe the lamentable results of parental ties in others. They will not grow powerful or rich for fear of corruption. In this way they confess, to a greater degree than the conservative, the poverty of their philosophy. Cannot the mocking opponent legitimately say that if these apostles of a faith so dread to fall, how will they cope with a society of ordinary people, bound to love, to become parents, to attain positions of comparative power and wealth even under a socialist *régime*? Is it not better, whispers this devil's advocate, to keep to a system that allows for unchanging human nature? One by one, as they reach maturity the revolutionaries and the reformers assent and slink over to the enemy. A vague ideal cannot stand if not backed by a constructive philosophy.

Such a philosophy the Marxian Communist therefore claims to supply. He views himself as a scientific politician assisting a predetermined economic march of history. He is a dogmatist, like any other, but a scientist, no. Having discovered the profound influence which economic circumstances exercise upon the beliefs of mankind, he builds entirely on this hypothesis without regard to other relevant facts. He has noticed the beliefs inspired by hunger and insecurity, but not those which spring from sex and parenthood, from the influence of scientific thought, or from traditional conceptions of life that have no application to present economic conditions. The hold of Christianity over the imagination, the connection between parenthood and property, the confusion about the position and character of women, all these he will pass by, or attempt to solve solely by economic deliverance. I do not deny the importance of solving economic problems, but their solution is not a panacea for all the ills from which humanity is suffering. When nations, classes, or women are oppressed, sympathy leads their champions to suppose that they will of necessity use freedom rightly ; but once they are free their defects as well as their qualities begin to appear. Thus we are driven back on a right understanding and guidance of human nature. It is significant for the Marxian doctrine that Marx developed his ideas before the evolutionary theory or the coming of modern physics and psychology. His followers are dominated by the special skill required in mechanics, whose imaginative picture derives from Descartes' " Give me matter and motion and I will construct the world ". The Christian thought of God or of the ruler at work in the universe with his hands [1] in personal relation

[1] The disappearance of the hand as an intermediary between man and the things he creates is of considerable importance in our imaginative picture of society, and the relation of mind to matter.

245

with his subjects, the industrially minded
thinks of Him in a power station at the heart
of a complex mechanical structure. The
industrialist believes you can make society as
you make a machine. You draw the plans one
day, manufacture the parts, fit them together,
and behold a world where formerly there was
nothing, a world which is the creation of your
mind. That a different technique is required
in dealing with flesh and blood, intellect and
imagination, from that applied to iron and
steel, rods and pistons, does not seem to cross
the mind of the typical captain of industry,
be he capitalist or socialist. That in human
individuals and communities there is a
phenomenon called growth, and a spontaneous
or instinctive activity does not occur to these
people. Machines do not grow and confine
their activity to making regular motions when
you wind them up. Fundamentally this view
of life cuts into animal vigour quite as severely
as religious asceticism. Human beings are to
become orderly, efficient, industrious. The
plans are made, the clockwork ready, fit
everybody in, turn the key, and behold the
millennium. Everybody does his work, must

not drink, takes sex as a necessity like food, and gives his offspring to the State experts to bring up. In such a society the life of instinct disappears as surely as it does in a system of Christian repression. It is not driven underground, but made trivial and external to the personality. The State receives the devotion formerly paid to God and the life of the individual is swallowed up in that of the community. Yet there is no spontaneous generosity in this submersion. Each little individual goes on, tight and tidy, thin and metallic, doing his piece of work, taking his little pleasures, and wondering what is the mysterious hunger and discontent burning his inmost soul. I feel this in modern people. I do not know whether they feel it in themselves. There is a certain thwarted savagery and fierceness abroad among them, which derives from something deeper than their economic wrongs. The cynic might say it is the inevitable reaction of the beast in man against each civilization he has created. One by one he needs must tear them down, relapse into barbarism and build again. I do not believe this theory of history, though I do believe that times like our own are fraught with danger. Let savagery break loose, or panic, and in a flood a thousand modern forms of ancient superstition will be upon us—science persecuted, civilization decried. It is because our civilizations repeatedly deny instinct and the anarchic impulses of human nature that they come down in disaster. The one which has admitted them to a small degree, the Chinese, has survived shocks and storms for thousands of years and is not even destroyed from without because it civilizes its conquerors.

The mechanical synthesis may thus be as dangerous to happiness as the Christian. What remains ? Shall we go back to the patriarchal system, or to the anarchy postulated by the philosophers as the natural state of man ? All that we need is to study a little more carefully the human creature for whom societies are made and insist upon his right to happiness. Every administrator seems to forget when he rises to power that institutions are made to serve human life, not human life to serve institutions. Thus our imperialists are at present engaged on the education of the house-wife in eating imperially. The poor instinctive common-sensical creature so far has only considered quality, pleasantness, low prices in the food she consumes. Thus the imperial adventurers lament in the columns of the London *Times*. Noble souls, of course, eat from pure reason or from patriotism, but not because they enjoy or are hungry. What incredible folly possesses us that we go on believing in our capacity to live either like disembodied spirits or motor-cars? This movement from puritanical religion (which helped to make industrialism possible) to mechanical dogmas is leading us straight to disaster.

Two characteristics of the human structure especially merit our attention—its need of rest and its capacity for growth. Human activity is not regular and continuous, but spasmodic. Our faculties whether mental or physical are employed with impulsive concentration for a period and then relax for rest. Each period of concentration is directed in a primitive person by some imperative desire—one of those we have analysed in preceding chapters. The effort of will which we make to concentrate when we do not so desire is a sophistication which experience has constructed. We know that the result of the activity and the feeling of achievement will be pleasant, though the immediate activity may bore us. This applies to work in getting food, or learning, to some aspects of parenthood, but not to sex.

Our organization of society must therefore take full advantage of our active moments and allow plenty of freedom for rest, or recuperation through the employment of other faculties. So to organize life that we simply go on and on, day in, day out, at some regular monotony, never breaking out, never changing our environment, scarcely resting, is to make sure that the pent-up energies which for a time seek their outlet in dreams, pictures, stories of lives more adventurous and lovely than our own, will ultimately burst forth in savagery to destroy the whole mechanism of external discipline. The specialization of work which is a feature of industrial civilization absolutely demands short hours, and an education of the personality such that each individual will find a thousand spontaneous and delightful occupations in his leisure time. Otherwise that vague sense of maladjustment, of being cheated of we know not what—which comes of thwarted instinct—will leave us an easy prey to the fiercest and basest passions when occasion arises.

A human being is not a set piece with so many rods and screws but an organism constantly growing in complexity. Every impression the human structure receives during growth will either assist or impair its capacity for work, life and happiness. There does come a point in the life of an individual where no further additions can be attracted to the growing crystal of his mind, when his mental faculties stiffen just as his muscles do. When this point is reached a man or woman does become in a way mechanical, a dancing doll that can only make certain movements and utter certain thoughts. Do we not know the phenomenon in peppery colonels, parsons, and doctrinaire socialists? In people whose education has been rigid and restricted, this point is reached earlier than in those to whom all horizons have been freely opened. It would be rash to set the term of years that elasticity continues. Each one of us, growing older, pushes the limit just beyond the age himself has reached. To people of advancing years the impressions stored in memory are precious, just as to long established communities traditions are, often quite unconsciously, a cherished possession. Do not communities grow weary, and their institutions so stiff and hoary that they must die completely before new life is possible ? I do not think so. Only our stupidity and impatience lead us to adopt this counsel of despair. Each generation springing fresh is capable of modifying without destroying its environment, provided the elders do not hamper it by false education. One thing we must all stamp into our minds before we grow quite stiff and set in our ways and that is our duty to the younger generation. If we want the life of man to go forward on the path of discovery and invention then we do not desire upheavals that bring barbarism in their train. Therefore the generations that follow us must not be driven to fierce revolt before they can achieve their desires. Nor must we set barriers to the liberation of an oppressed sex or class. The more cunning among our reactionaries perceive this. Where formerly they could by authority and oppression mould the rebels or the young to their antiquated philosophy, now they are at pains to inculcate it by insidious flattery and the bribery which the pleasures of wealthy society can provide. As each rebel emerges they fasten upon him urging their sincere desire for social betterment and the similarity of their views with his own. This change of tactic implies a doubt and an anxiety in the minds of those who pursue it. In the divisions of Reuben there are great searchings of heart. People begin to admit that persuasion is more powerful than authority. This makes it the more urgent that we should not reply to reaction by force and asceticism, which are its own time-honoured weapons. Rather must we by clear exposition of a human philosophy shake to the last stones their crazy foundations. Upon us who believe that all human beings can live for happiness and creation lies the burden of convincing our fellow-men and women by our actions as much as by our thoughts and words.

We have to face the utter falsity of the old psychology and dig deep until the springs of human life and happiness are found. We ourselves must first live by instinct and by intelligence, weaving them closely together in the conduct of our lives. In this way we shall learn for ourselves that mechanism and repression are not the secrets of happiness for individuals and therefore not to be imposed by States. We shall go on to rebuild the human animal who has been so shamefully distorted and encompass him with all that he needs to grow in wisdom and in splendour. We shall not emulate the ignorant gardeners who place water-loving plants upon a parched and desert hill and scold their excessive lust for water as a mortal sin. Growth is to be handled with science and not with superstition. Here, again, the gulf yawns between the agricultural mystic and the evolutionist. To me it seems more and more impossible for those who love humanity to come to terms with any form of Christianity. Broad-minded Christians may feel that the full human life for which we are hungry is preached in many sayings scattered through the Gospels, but to me the method of approach is wrong from the start. Even in the Sermon on the Mount there is very little which I can whole-heartedly accept as a basis for individual and social action. And what is good in it has been ruined by the interpretations of established Churches and preachers. Assuredly we do not live by bread alone, but neither can the words of God in Scripture or in the mouths of his preachers suffice us.

The preaching of poverty, stoicism and suffering as a State religion leads to a denial not only of wisdom, but of bread also to the starving. Generous co-operation cannot spring from duty, nor all-embracing love of our fellow-men from purely spiritual sources What we feel about the world must be built upon something deeply embedded in our physical nature, love of the soil, the water, the air, love of a mate, love of our children. The Jewish patriarchal system which Christ corrected by a greater insistence on individual rather than racial salvation had in it in my belief the more natural source of communal co-operation.[1] Clearly the problem of building a human society is always the difficulty of establishing a relation between individual and communal happiness. The method of the Christian was to give to the individual a promise

---

[1] Even to-day Jewish people are notoriously better than Christians in caring for their children.

of spiritual happiness and of immortality for himself and those he loved, in return for a life of private and public duty here on earth. Yet I believe that the intractable selfishness of modern individuals, so lamented by religious people, derives more from their teaching than from the materialism or hedonism which they condemn. Man is not by his animal nature as selfish as theories of spiritual virtue have made him. Love tears at his ego through the intensity of a physical delight which demands the companionship of another creature, and expansion in parenthood draws him on to greater devotion. Rivalry and insecurity, it is true, rouse him to jealousy and angry defiance, and the task of the moralist and the politician is to make these perversions unnecessary. But to proceed by a warning against the snares of the flesh is to dry the springs of good as well as of evil, and enclose him in a colourless ego from which only by duty can you drive him forth. What use is it to command men to love their enemies who, through walking the prescribed paths of virtue, have never whole-heartedly loved wife, children, or friends? I do not mean loved with spiritual grace and compassion, but with a physical sympathy flooding every nerve of the body by which pain and danger to another is quite literally pain to ourselves. The family love which we find in the Fairchild family, or the letters of Dr. Arnold, never had this supreme quality, because by Christian teaching the soul must be abandoned primarily to God and not to human creatures. Theoretically the love of God flooding our being should have spilled over into our dealings with men. But this is psychologically unsound. In actual fact the human soul cannot express itself in the realm of pure spirit, it does not expand upwards into a rarer atmosphere, rather does it become arid and withered because religion has severed it from the instinct which is its root. The desire to keep the personality intact displayed by enormous numbers of men and women in their relations with lovers, with their children and with the community derives ultimately from the notion that the individual was dedicated to God alone. It is reinforced by the mechanistic theory in which the important relation is between the individual and the State for which he or she works, and which in return gives liberty and the necessaries

257

of life. Freedom—economic independence, why do they not spell happiness? Where instinct is starved they never will, and never can. Nor, while instinct is starved, will co-operation between human beings be anything but compulsion and duty. We can no more live by pure reason than by faith. When for instance the strong instincts of sex and parenthood batter at the natural egoism or philosophy of many modern men and women they recoil in anxiety and fear. Not only do a thousand social and economic barriers obstruct, but individuals have been trained rather to resistance than acceptance. They cry out that they are drowning, that they will not be enslaved to another human being or to children. It is a weakness, menial, inferior, to be swept under by the tide of sexual or family love. It will destroy the mind, dwarf the imagination. And so they embark upon a struggle for self-preservation in which neither mind, nor love, nor happiness can long survive. Sipping, sampling, dallying on the brink, they dare not drink deep in the fiery goblet, nor plunge head foremost into the glowing waters. Many that are in horror of contraceptives for the body carry the most virulent contraceptives in their souls. Not for them that magical fertilization of the soul which springs of perfect sex union, that opening of the lonely heart and mind in love to another, that quickening of every thought and every pulse to renewed and powerful activity. Struggling against submersion in love and defending a false idea of personal integrity, they miss the easy way to bind their happiness to the happiness of others —the simple link of acute physical sympathy in joy or in pain.

If it is a slavery to feel every wound to those we love like a dagger at our own hearts, it is at least a slavery easy of acceptance, abounding in happiness for ourselves, and fertile in its possibilities for a communal philosophy. I know of nothing more likely to transform society than that men and women should love one another without stint or fear, and unashamedly yield to the physical tenderness they feel for each other and their children. Let these emotions rather than glory, grandeur, virtue, or riches enlist their intelligence in private and public life.

There has never been a time in human

history when men and women, both free creatures, have been free to love without the coarseness or triviality engendered by ignorant superstition. The love that to-day is open to all men and women of intelligence and physical vitality was unknown in any race or epoch of the past, save to rare and exceptional people. Invariably, love has been enslaved to religious superstition, to a misguided view of woman, or to the function of parenthood. Egypt, Greece, Rome, China, medieval and modern Europe, the refinements of chivalrous love, of eighteenth century intrigue, everywhere it is the same story. Sex love as an end in itself is always despised, or where indulged, felt to be wicked. The love of mating, even at its best, is no more than a prelude to a too heavy burden of parental responsibility, bringing in its train all the bitter passions that attend the threat of starvation and rivalry to the parents and their offspring. Let love be free at last and sex the perfect instrument which it might be for profound mutual understanding and co-operation for happiness. Let children come where they are loved and in numbers that do not overtax parental strength and tenderness.

Let our social system be so built as not merely to condone, but explicitly to allow sexual freedom to all men and women. Where neither patriarchal families nor the God-given authority of kings and priests dominate, no other course is open to us. A democratic society is only great and free in so far as greatness and freedom breathe from the individuals that compose it. In such a society, women cannot be slaves : they, too, must be free if their minds and bodies are to be magnificent in work, in love, and in the creation of children. It is not only impossible but criminal to stop short of sex in the emancipation of men and women. But such an emancipation must be real, not pretended. We must incorporate it in our laws, not merely pay it lip-service. When sex as a free delight is open to all, it will be open to very few as a career. No man or woman is to have sexual rights over another, nor economic claims. Children alone are to be protected and their lives made secure. Every kind of matrimonial arrangement should be allowed, provided there is no compulsion and the children are well cared for by the parents or by experts. The jealousies and hatreds which attend our present system would for a time continue, but disappear gradually in response to certain changes. It would really make a very great difference if wives could neither be held as property, nor supported in childless idleness. It would make a difference if a few wealthy women were to assert their right to have a matriarchal family with several fathers to demonstrate the absurdity of conforming to one pattern or the other.

But if we remove all the economic reasons for monogamy there still remains a slender instinctive justification for it when children are involved. To co-operate over the care of children is a very great joy to a man and woman, even where there is no distinction of function such as the father being breadwinner and the mother practising the domestic arts. I believe the majority of people desirous of children would turn to this finally, but it would be a mistake if it were their only ideal at the start, for poverty of instinctive experience is a thing above all others to be avoided if we want happy individuals and a happy society.

It is to be hoped that from maternity centres

and nursery schools there may gradually spread upwards a more maternal attitude to the whole of education and that men and women, at last combining as equals over their children, may also combine in public activity and come to regard education not as the driving in of a little necessary knowledge and a lot of imperialist or class war propaganda, but rather as a deliberate creation of the future of mankind. I have tried to show that education, especially in early years, may be very positive without indulging in propaganda. We have to safeguard the children until they are harmonious characters from the strife, disputes and insecurity that infest the adult world. Let them at a later age decide whether they will admire the British Empire and Australian mutton and Canadian beef, or discover for themselves that the *bourgeoisie* and anarchists are so wicked that they must all be killed. Clearly it is to the present advantage of rulers to train docile and warlike citizens, but I do not at all despair as the methods of modern psychology are explained, of getting agreement on the eradication of fear, hatred, and destruction from the child's view of life. Such agreement will lead in the long run to a more humane attitude to the adult population. I believe that the great mass of people, after the experience of the laſt ten years, do in their heart of hearts desire security and peace and would not be sorry to see emerging a morality that could bring these about and from them proceed to a morality of positive creation. The importance of security in dealing with the perversions of inſtinēt can scarcely be over-eſtimated. If we are assured deep in our inſtinēt of the very great love of an individual towards ourselves we are not jealous of love given by that individual to others. Again, it is the conscious and unconscious memory of paſt oppression, miseducation and ſtarvation which makes us militant and grasping in our parental funētions. When we or our anceſtors have known this torture we seek by hook or by crook to avert it from our children. When we know that we can get work and food for ourselves the hatred that used to kill rivals diminishes to a little back-biting or a friendly competition and may even disappear ın co-operation. When we can reach inter-national agreement about necessary supplies, and the size of populations, as we can very soon by steady persistence in that direction, group rivalry will cease to be the devastating thing which it is at present. To rely only on economic security in this last respect would, however, be folly. The impulse to national aggression springs also from atavistic fears and the religious superstitions built upon them. It arises also where individuals in a nation are starved or twisted in the deep creative functions of parenthood and sex. It is no mere accident that Christianity is a good fighting religion and that the deeply instinctive parental civilization of China is pacific. I would like to see a generation of children spend their early lives away from insecurity and anxiety in democratic child communities where the creative impulses to work, knowledge, and imagination were actively encouraged. Knowledge about sex and parenthood would of course be imparted. I believe that such a generation would demand of their later life what early environment had given them, and that they would not rest content until they had bent their energies to achieving this result. I believe that as lovers and parents they would act as their early training had led them to act in learning and in play. Filled to the brim with delight in creative activity and the skill to indulge it they would find neither room nor time for the silly perversions and preoccupations that at present distort the majority of lives.

If I insist pre-eminently upon sex and parenthood in this argument, it is because these are strong instincts in almost all men and women, capable of bringing great joy and at present the source of much misunderstanding and unhappiness. The reactionary will argue that on my premises we need only to return to pure agriculture and a patriarchal life to make everybody happy. Artists, men of science, celibate women workers may feel that I have under-estimated knowledge, or the delight of self-expression in work or play unconnected with sex and children.

On the contrary, I believe intelligence and knowledge to be of the most vital importance. Intelligence without instinct is futile, undirected instinct beats the air. Instinct is the spring and skill and intelligence the channel. Not a moral superiority to animals, but rather intelligence

and inherited knowledge are the mark of the
human species. I do not mean pure reason
guiding and curbing the passions in an
eighteenth century sense, but an acquired
skill which determines the direction in which
the passions shall flow. The mechanistic
theory of society shows all too clearly the
dangers of eighteenth century psychology and
science. But I do not wish to see the industrial
system destroyed despite its dangers to human
happiness because it is the expression of
intelligence applied to the solution of excessive
work. It is an instrument of the physical
comfort of the great mass of people. In the
same way medicine expresses the application
of intelligence to diminishing pain, postponing
death and decay, and probably, as we advance,
actually improving our physical strength and
beauty. A primitive life without science is
not the best means either to health or instinctive
happiness. It means overwork and disease,
whose ravages are increased by too great
exposure to the severities of hard weather,
dirt, bad housing, and hunger. On the other
hand a wrong theory of man's nature leading
to civilizations based on false values produces

the idleness, overfeeding, and frivolity which destroy even the happiness of the so-called fortunate few. It may well be, that with a more just view of the relation of mind and body we shall use science to make us superb and strong rather than to provide remedies ; or overheated houses for people who have forgotten how to walk in open spaces and expose their bodies to the sun.

Then again, a primitive life imprisons women in instinct to the great detriment of their happiness and the health and characters of their children. I am not content to leave the ignorant conservative so-called maternal woman in sole possession of the home, any more than to submit to purely male dominance outside it. The mind of a woman is necessary to civilization and just as a mother now develops maternal instinct by acquired facility in the mechanical care of children, bathing them, putting on and off and making their clothes, so might she develop that instinct as a faculty shot through and through with scientific intelligence, thus making of maternity a work of supreme physical and psychological creation.

These are in a sense utilitarian aspects of the use of intelligence, but knowledge as an end in itself is important. In the study of mathematics, physics, astronomy, chemistry, the human being is momentarily divorced from the instinctive texture of his life, except in so far as we may say that all these pursuits arise from the primitive curiosity formerly associated with danger, the search for food and sex. In applying the intellect to pure science man is more free of emotional influence than in the less disciplined flights of imagination which he expresses in the arts. To kill the promptings of instinct in art would be to destroy art itself. It is true that artistic expression may be highly charged with intellect, for instance delight in pure or significant form is the aesthetic pleasure of intellectual types. But such forms of art are not necessarily more pure or noble than the direct expression of simple emotions any more than the work of the physicist is more pure or noble than the work of a capable mother. It is a different kind of creative activity, that is all. These moral judgments are out of place in estimating the value of the creative work of individuals.

Creation is the supreme thing whatever the
stuff or medium on which it is employed.
It is not finer to be a competent private
secretary than to work on a poultry farm, nor
is it nobler to write bad novels than produce
and nurture excellent babies.

Many who are free of Christian beliefs are
still so well tutored in ascetic values as to set
the worship of pure intelligence untrammelled
by debasing emotion in the place of the
worship of virtue or of God. Glorious indeed
and worthy of admiration are the minds
which through the ages have hurled against
persecution and darkness the fiery battalions
of thought, blown gently upon the spark of
human reason, tenderly fanned and nursed
it into a beacon fire. Great indeed is the
ecstasy of those rare beings that in some
secret corner of our material world, unknown
perhaps, unrecognized, put out some hard-
won calculation, some strange perplexing
thought, nebulous it may be at first even to
themselves, but when understood changing
the whole material world and the life and
imagination of posterity for ever. Such people
need no philosophy of joy or of despair to

make them content to have lived out their span of human existence ; and the contemplation of their souls and of their handiwork will ever be to lesser men and women an ecstasy of reverence and love.

None the less such exaltation may and does lead to superstition. Great though thought be, it is by instinct that the majority of mankind are rightly bound to live. Neither to assert too boldly nor under-estimate the claims of humdrum men and women is really not too difficult a task. To say that the creative thinker or artist is not morally superior to ourselves, that there is no higher or lower activity, is not to say that our system should make impossible these rare and wonderful lives. Here I touch what I began to say about quality and quantity in my first chapter. Ordinary men and women, all of us, would be better employed in building a system to free and intensify intelligence than in envious suppression or in vain prayers and shrines to the noble army of martyrs in the past. We would be better employed in perfecting our own intelligence and applying it creatively to the roughest and hardest work, than in sighing for a world of idle contemplation where we should be free of the eternal bondage to the needs and impulses of the body. Thought is neither our servant, nor we its abject slaves. Thought is creation, but the manner of its use by the undiscerning may render it sterile. It must not be used as the Christians have used it to bind and fetter and poison every free bodily activity, nor to hew and chop and propel matter in the shape of men, women, and machines through a well-organized universe. Let thought flow through our instincts as the water floods and recedes in the deep caverns of the sea, let it breathe through them as our measured breath rises and falls and sustains our living body. What has this to do with happiness, or with modern civilization ? Everything. The great and fundamental unhappiness of man, the falsity of his attempts at civilization spring from his inability to harmonize the life of instinct with his new developed life of reason. He cannot bring himself to understand that these two lives have not two sources human and divine, one lower, one higher, but that both arose in harmony in his own nature and can in harmony meet once more. He cannot bring himself to believe that mind and matter are not separate principles, but both the same and the very stuff of which he and his universe are made. That matter is not solid lumps but tenuous and shifting, that mind is not pure spirit but a construction with a physical basis come dimly over to modern men and women from the discoveries of science. Perhaps this knowledge may at last persuade them to believe—what long since common sense might have taught them—that the secret of happiness is the fusion of the mental and bodily life both in the individual and the community.

We are now perhaps in a position to define what is meant by civilization as modern men and women may understand it. It is not the striking of a balance between body and mind as classical thought proposed, nor yet the neglect or subjugation of the body in the interest of spiritual fervour, which was the Christian view. Nor can it be reached by a materialist view of society which has not fully understood the nature and needs of human organisms, and which has approached without science and only with moral and class prejudice the problem of quality versus quantity.

Civilization in the original and strict sense of the word meant the conforming of human life to the town type of environment because in that environment habits were more complex and intelligence more lively. Thus it recognized the part to be played by the mind in the process. Religion, in particular Christianity as we know it, is quite useless for our purpose. Not only has it never claimed and never attempted to assist communal civilization (except in so far as it carried forward the heritage of the constructive Empire of Rome), it has been actively hostile to exact scientific knowledge that is giving rise to modern civilization. Christianity merely claimed to make men and women good by prohibitions and dreams. Under its influence nearly all of us conceive of civilization as a state of society in which the moral nature of man governs his instincts and the use of his knowledge. Science, we say, is bankrupt unless directed by the virtue of men. The truth is that the virtue of men is bankrupt because it is not informed by instinct and by science. We should reverse our whole process and let instinct working through a technique perfected by science govern or rather create men's moral nature. Civilizing does not proceed by imposing moral prohibitions on coarse and raw instinct, but by rendering the instinctive life more supple and varied in its expression through a great variety of habits learnt by intelligence. The development of speech from guttural and rough noises to the delicate flexibility of modern language is an example of the procedure. That change has been accompanied by a corresponding refinement of the jaw formation and the skull. Slowly and with difficulty the acquired thought of one generation takes its place as a part of the almost instinctive technique of another. Science makes the technique, instinct supplies the energy, and that technique in its turn by a slow and gradual process becomes so fused with instinct that it is almost indistinguishable from it. In this way instinct itself very gradually changes. The inheritance of acquired characteristics is not yet held and proved by evolution in animal parentage, but it is clear, I think, as a social phenomenon. We may be said to have acquired certain industrial and agricultural habits which we hand on, almost without teaching them directly, to our children. Similarly, modern practices in education, in many teachers almost instinctive, are the product of the theories of men like Rousseau in the past. A new technique of child nurture for young children will in like manner probably modify the expression of parental love in subsequent generations. We have to be on our guard against the whole traditional theory of moral education. An attempt to impose a discipline which too severely represses strong desires at any given period in the life of individuals or communities will always be met in the last resort by revolt and destruction. But knowledge which can assist and vary the activities of deep-planted desires will always be accepted and absorbed. Thus the means to scientific murder are joyfully developed by a community whose tribal passions have been carefully fostered by the traditional moralists. Moral education of individual and community can only proceed by providing facilities and an intelligent apparatus for the use of those instincts which make for life rather than destruction. Liberate motherhood, for example, and make it an important work that no one but a fool will despise and to which the best will aspire. But if you set about training and encouraging the mother in the spirit of the old morality, and command her, as a moral principle applied to herself, not to slap her child, she will not refrain when a burst of anger seizes her. On the other hand an intelligent knowledge of child nurture so well understood that it is part of her maternal nature will really lead to right action even under provocation.

Human happiness, the pursuit of knowledge, the expression of emotion in art should be the objects of civilization and the aim of the politician. We may add to this art and science applied to the problem of human personality, by which we may create human beings of greater beauty, greater health, greater knowledge than those which people our present world. I do not mean by this imposing the state's idea of happiness upon all, or state art, or state-controlled knowledge, still less do I mean that science be applied to human nature in order to create docility in the citizens.

Everything that is lovely, intelligent, vital in communal life comes to it through the intensity of life in individuals. The function of the state is merely to set men free and settle the background against which singly and in free co-operation men and women will continue consciously and unconsciously the evolutionary process. Religious people, moralists, politicians, one and all abdicate before the problem of human nature, and invent some device or set of absurd beliefs for avoiding the difficult facts. Science, they tell us, has nothing to say about human nature, the facts of race, geography, original sin are unchangeable. Others lament that men ought to be good, and yet somehow they are not. Patience and knowledge are applied by us to building a railway engine, but when it comes to building a man or a human society, we think impatient bullying and ignorance the best methods. How about a little historical vision, a little accurate medical knowledge, a little psychology for a change ? Men and women who sit in Parliaments have great power over the happiness of millions of human beings. Yet we demand of them less skill and knowledge of human nature

than we demand that a farm labourer know
about pigs, or a mechanic about the engine
which he drives. Of man they know nothing
but what their prejudices may have taught
them, unless it be how to play upon the baser
passions of the herd in political speech, press,
and war propaganda.

To build a society upon knowledge of human
nature and its needs implies much greater
changes than many people suppose. It does
not mean merely taking a broad human view
and perpetuating casual animal life in individual
units and family groups. Though it is necessary
to emphasize the difference between the
organic life of a human personality and the
exact life of a machine, it is also necessary to
understand the chemical and psychological
processes which build that organic life and
personality. To do this we must not continue
to treat each individual as a unit, and then
try to resolve the relation of that unit to society.
We should not begin with the family group,
nor the individual soul, nor yet the economic
man. These, as I have tried to show, have been
the three stages we have passed through in
solving the problem of social co-operation.

The first was built upon a solid biological basis, but cannot be applied without great modification to very large societies. The second is the Christian theory, whose disadvantages have already been sufficiently discussed. The third sums up the rationalist position, which has steadily lost ground since the war, and is being discarded by many people for a semi-religious view of life. When they discover that self-interest and economic security are not the most important human motives, many people seem to receive a shock which drives them to seek a religious sanction for morals. They hark back to self-denial, discipline, service, an exalted life of the spirit, as opposed to the worship of things material.[1] For instance, Mr. Aldous Huxley, who in common with most of us finds eighteenth century rationalism inadequate, must needs start maintaining that religions, which are the worst enemy of biological needs, are expressions of the Life Force, and serve its purposes. The medieval spirit of Russia, speaking through modern jargon, is having a reactionary influence upon very many able

[1] *The Nation and Athenæum*, 24th April, 1926.

minds. Even Bernard Shaw goes about saying that the Russian schools, which make use of hate propaganda just like our own, are teaching the children the spirit of social co-operation.

Mr. Maynard Keynes is amazed to discover in Russia a society engaged in the steady eradication of the money motive from life. In actual fact the theory, though not the spirit, of that society, is a far more rigid insistence on the economic motive than is found in our own. The paradox of Russia is a medieval or Renaissance outlook wedded to an eighteenth century metaphysic and psychology. Russians believe with religious fervour that there is no soul and no God and no reality other than matter of an eighteenth century kind. But surely intelligent people have known for a long time that men or women who work only for money are hirelings, and that love of creating art, love of knowledge, love of mate, love of offspring, are as compelling and important motives of human action as the desire to keep alive or to have power. We do not need religion to reveal anything so obvious and self-evident as this. If only people would give up picking on one motive and then another and saying it must be bad, because fundamentally they believe that men and women are bad. Why not dispense with all this moral indignation? When we want a waterfall to generate electricity we do not say it is bad and wicked because we have to take some trouble to persuade it to do the work. Why not try the same attitude with man in society? Treat his aptitudes and desires like the rushing water as data that are given, and that we do not judge but utilize with skill. We should even give up thinking of a human being as a character enclosed within a body. Neither the body nor the mind are give as units. Both are changing constantly in interaction with the outside world. The important facts in life are the responses of the body to stimulae, or of the mind to images and memories, not the existence of that individual mind or that individual body itself.

Indeed, we cannot say that that body exists, except that we perceive a more or less constant shape, or the repetition of certain chemical processes that maintain it. Similarly the personality or mind does not exist apart from all the memories, associations, and images that compose it. I mean this in a literal, not a mystic sense. If people would study young children and modern psychology, they would soon see that there are not good men and bad men, but merely good or life-giving acts or events, or bad or death-dealing acts or events.[1] When a speaker inspires a crowd, it is neither the speaker nor the crowd that matters, but the clash of the two, the emotion generated by that clash, and its results in mental or physical action. The same analysis can be applied to an artist playing an instrument or to the relations of lovers, parents, and children; of students to the ideas which stir them, nations to the words that move them. Everything in the world moves, falls, combines like the patterns of the kaleidoscope, the momentary suspension of the pattern is what matters, not the intrinsic character of each little bit of coloured glass.

Legislation and education therefore should aim at producing the greatest possible number of life-giving events, and the least possible number of death-dealing ones. To do this we must carefully study the building of human bodies and of human minds, not as things isolated and

[1] Double personality is an illustration of this thesis.

complete, but in the closest relation to their
environment. We should try to forget that the
body is solid and think of the electrons that
dance to make it, of its response to light and
warmth, to cool or bitter winds, of the constant
interchange and fusion between it and the
sunlight and the air, of the rhythmic pattern of
its motion in walking, running, and dancing.
A precisely similar pattern of events, fusions,
interactions, is the human mind.[1] Education
and legislation should not deal with creating
good people or clever personalities, indeed,
they should scarcely aim at creating personality
at all. Since each person is a somewhat
haphazard bundle of needs and impulses, it
is the needs and impulses rather than the
individual that we must stress. Every possible
human need and impulse must be given an
opportunity in early training, and opportunity
preserved for the exercise of every possible
human need and impulse in later life.
Specialization may be imposed by the necessity
for organizing work, but richness of life,
intricacy of pattern, which make for lasting
happiness, are best achieved by postponing

[1] Cf. definition of human being. Chap. III.

as long as possible the setting of mental, physical or emotional aptitudes in a mould or a groove. The trend of our education of young children at present is to accept this theory, but it is not accepted in our organization of society. This is largely because our society is no longer, like the Chinese, a biological group, but organized for mutual interest and the division of work. For this reason we stress the particular mental or physical aptitude by which an individual makes his living, rather than the whole of his intellectual or instinctive life.[1] For this reason also, as well as by religious suppression of animal life, we have lost that instinctive co-operation that is well known to exist among primitive peoples. To group people according to their skill as doctors, carpenters, bricklayers, teachers, etc., is probably the first step towards legislating and educating for separate human needs and impulses rather than to produce the good men required by religion. The next stage is to dissolve individuals altogether and to educate for chains or series of " good " reactions of

---

[1] This is one of the defects of trade unionists in their attitude to social problems.

instinct and intellect, that is to say to call forth
in every situation love, creativeness, generosity,
intelligent interest rather than the opposite
of these emotions. The life of a human being
is simply a series of manifestations of this kind,
it is just as if he were playing a tune, or tracing
a pattern. But the relation of his mental and
physical structure to these manifestations is
more intimate than that of a violin to a tune or
crayon to a drawing. In a sense he *is* the tune
or pattern. Education and opportunity arrange
the sequence of the notes he will play
throughout life or the pattern which his
thoughts and actions will trace. Chance throws
together the *genes* which determine his
hereditary aptitudes. It is therefore simpler
and more accurate to say that the community
should aim at producing health, strength,
artistic and intellectual effort; skilled workman-
ship, and sturdy physical labour ; lovely and
complete sex unions, generous and creative
parenthood ; rather than to say that we aim
at producing virtuous or even well-developed
men and women. We must get from men and
women what we can ; if we are too ready
with moral correctives of their imperfections

we may choke or whittle away the good things they might have given us. Each should do creatively whatever he is doing at any given moment, regardless of whether it is consistent with his character. So intense and so instinctive should be this creativeness from moment to moment that it leaves no time nor thought for moral censure of oneself or neighbours. Instead of feeling " I, who am a good and wonderful man, paint this picture or write this poem, and so-and-so, next door, wastes his time and does neither ", we should feel " this picture is being painted, this poem written ", and the next moment pass to loving our children and pulling them out of the fender. Such are the manifestations for which laws and education should provide.

It is far more difficult and complex to do this than to make good men and women, but it is the road to happiness. Good men think only of their account with God and reck nothing of their contact with their fellow creatures and the universe. Opportunists and pragmatists see only their bodily acts and their outward consequences, oblivious of the complex structure which is called the inner life. To those who cannot see man but as a part of his physical environment, and who yet find in the gossamer threads of thought, of beauty, and of love a reality as certain as the clang of the hammer upon the anvil, the distinction between thoughts and acts, internal and external events is meaningless. No thought, no act, no emotion of the child is unimportant, because out of all these things the life and the habits of the adult and so the life and habits of our world are made.

So having passed from the expansive happiness of instinctive animal life to the tidy and close-knit self which we struggle to maintain intact among a thousand disruptive physical and intellectual forces, with what joyful freedom and abandonment we now melt and dissolve again into our background—dancing electrons, puffs of air and light, dewdrop chains of instincts, actions, thoughts, emotions ; happiest when of all these elements there is not one that must lie in shadow or in cold, or lose his freshness from too greedy drinking of the sun, but all may gleam and quiver to the light of day.

As we look around us we see on all sides

innumerable men and women whom the old methods of religion, morals, and politics have failed to subdue to duty or to turn to creative and happy lives. Why not try a new inspiration, new politics, new morality ? Not an easy and hastily devised formula that will bring power and popularity to its advocates, can perhaps be imposed for a time and then must perish in bloodshed like the harsh and superficial formulae of the past, but something that is deep, life-giving, capable of standing the shock of battle, of misrepresentation, even of defeat ? A philosophy that expands to new knowledge, that the ages to come will enrich but cannot destroy. People cry out for belief, for happiness, for comfort in disaster. Can we give it to them without the falsehoods, the prohibitions, the empty promises on which in the past they have been fed ? I say that we can. I say that if we do not, we stand in great peril. I say that life itself gives us the answer to life's riddles, and the universe itself holds the key to its mysteries. We can give to men and women not vague ideals of humanitarianism, not easy dreams of dull and spiritless utopias, but set before their feet here and now the path of glorious destiny whose treading is abundant life and happiness to themselves and abundant life and happiness to their posterity. Teach men and women that life is creation, that thought and imagination are creation, their fusion and incarnation in instinct the mechanism of life itself, that each life is only valuable in so far as it uses and uses to the full every creative activity which it possesses, that dreams are of the stuff of the universe, to be woven into separate and corporate lives as the artist struggles to speak through a material medium, and as the inventor seeks the mathematical formula for his machine. Every one of us in some aspect of life could be creator, artist, scientist, with a different technique according as our material was steel, clay, paint, human nature. Urging us on we should have a creative vitality built upon bodily health and a soul delivered from fear. Here is a simple religion which mankind is now in a position to grasp. It has no need to postulate God. It is no barrier to individual happiness, it dispenses with the past discrepancies of virtue and vice, spirit and matter which have hitherto tormented us. It gives women as well as men

equality and freedom, it makes of work a
glory and a joy instead of a humiliation and a
misery. It unbinds from love the shackles of
repression and ignorance, bringing in their
place mutual ecstasy and enlightenment. Any
human being in whom this faith is burning
no matter what he touches, it turns to happiness and beauty in his hands. No matter
what problem he approaches, he will find
traditional politics and morals prowl about
him like the hosts of Midian on every side.
He need neither heed them nor destroy but
go forward. They will melt about him as the
snows upon the mountain beneath the summer
sun.

But what of death ? not of ourselves but those
we love, or the agony of loss and despair which
even in life may be our portion ? The misery
of loneliness after a vain search for companionship in love or understanding ? If
men and women were more free and their early
life and education more secure and harmonious,
there would be fewer jangled and disappointed
lovers, fewer heart-broken parents, fewer
desperate and rebellious sons and daughters.
In a community where instinctive happiness

was not rare nor suffering exalted, those whom great sorrow had visited would find some healing rather than ground for envy and malevolence in the happiness of their neighbours. Against death, disaster, and sorrow the skill and courage of all mankind would be mobilized. What we could do to avert danger and to master our environment we would do as a human society. Apart from that we must learn to meet death with quiet acceptance. Is our universe so limited, is our life so lacking in variety and mystery that we must run to take refuge in another world ? Here in the universe is our home and our kingdom, not ours only, or our children's, or our lover's, but belonging to all mankind. Whatever is lovely for a day, for an hour, for a moment has been worthy the effort that called it into being— a flower, music, poetry, a human being. To love the springing of fresh life must teach us that to die and to lose those human creatures who have been to us fountains of clear water, cloak and fireside in bleak weather, rest in weariness, eager life in moments of joy is our own individual sorrow that must not darken for us or for others the abundant life of the world.

Those we love live on for us in what they have given to our souls, we in what we have given to the souls of others, to children, to the young whom we may teach, to lovers ; we live in the words we have spoken or written for other men and women. We live in whatever mark of creation we have made and though it be small and unnoticed in the vastness of life, yet it may be as lovely as a common daisy staring cheerfully upwards among its fellows in a white-starred field. To brood on death is idle, it is the last stronghold of fear. Death's triumph is assured, we need therefore waste no time in morbid gloating on his victories. We want to defeat death, so far as in us lies, but the fear of death plays less and less part in determining our conduct and beliefs. Nor is it a source of so much unhappy thought as it used to be when judgment and hell-fire added to its terrors. We live our life, and do our work, that we must relinquish both in death matters nothing to the universe of which we are a part. That life goes on here, or anywhere, should be sufficient comfort for our individual loss. It is in its essence such a gallant phenomenon, beauty that perishes, life that dies that we are sustained and borne onward by an almost unwilling admiration in spite of our terrors. In any case, I do not believe that the threat of death disposes any men or women of strong impulses to regret life itself or not to live fully throughout their length of days, and I cannot agree with those who hold that any morality of happiness must break down before this final disaster. Nagging and grinding misery in earthly life, such misery as by common effort is preventable is the real root of religions of suffering. Hedonism demands a certain degree of security, but not more than we can give to all mankind if we so desire. Away with hypocrisies, timidities, doubts. Away with the darkness of ignorance. Let those men and women who know, who enjoy, and who are unafraid, open the prison gates for the rest of mankind. Let them teach and live, conquer public opinion, show that they can do better than those that traffic in the old wares of superstition and of hate. These feed upon destruction and despair, but they shall flourish on security and peace. Let such men and women build a human society in the image of human beings, vivid, warm, and quick with animal life, intricate and lovely in thought and emotion. Let this society have the natural grace and agility of an uncorseted body whose form springs from the play of living muscles, whose deftness and sure purpose arise from thought and action closely intertwined. Such a society, by virtue of its inner resilience, would have no need to meet danger, disease, and death with the external makeshifts of war, remedial artifice, and trumpery fables. Such a society, like the human beings that composed it, would be at home in the world, not fearing change but perpetually developing in suppleness and wisdom, perpetually devising new forms and new sources of delight.

Men and women, you have not only a right to such happiness, but the means to this happiness lie ready to your hand. Are they so simple that you must forever pass them by ?